The Last
Eve

and our end-time assignment

Susan Dunn

The Last Eve
© 2023 by Susan Dunn

Published by Insight International, Inc.
contact@freshword.com
www.freshword.com
918-493-1718

Unless otherwise noted all Scripture quotations are taken from the New King James Version®. Copyright © 1982 by Thomas Nelson. Used by permission. All rights reserved.

Scripture quotations marked (MSG) are taken from *THE MESSAGE,* copyright © 1993, 2002, 2018 by Eugene H. Peterson. Used by permission of NavPress. All rights reserved. Represented by Tyndale House Publishers, Inc.

Scripture quotations marked (AMP) are taken from the Amplified Bible, copyright © 2015 by The Lockman Foundation, La Habra, CA 90631. All rights reserved.

Scripture quotations marked (TPT) are from The Passion Translation®. Copyright © 2017, 2018, 2020 by Passion & Fire Ministries, Inc. Used by permission. All rights reserved. ThePassionTranslation.com.

Scripture quotations marked (CSB) are from The Christian Standard Bible. Copyright © 2017 by Holman Bible Publishers. Used by permission. Christian Standard Bible®, and CSB® are federally registered trademarks of Holman Bible Publishers, all rights reserved.

Scripture quotations marked (NIV) are from the Holy Bible, New International Version®, NIV®. Copyright © 1973, 1978, 1984, 2011 by Biblica, Inc.® Used by permission. All rights reserved worldwide.

ISBN: 978-1-943361-92-2
E-Book ISBN: 978-1-943361-93-9

Library of Congress Control Number: 2022903992

Printed in the United States of America.

Dedication

This book is dedicated to my husband, Derek, who has been instrumental to develop me to become the woman I am today. Thank you for showing our children and me how to love Jesus and follow Him.

Contents

Foreword

At one time or another, all of us have heard someone say, "We're in this mess, all because of Eve." Maybe it was said this way, "Because of Eve, we were cursed." These words and thoughts have caused women to always live under the imposed guilt of the first Eve. But is this true? What if this imposed guilt is a false accusation? What if we have misinterpreted the events in the Garden of Eden? What if there is another side to the story?

Eve was in the beginning and the Last Eve will be in the end. In this book, Susan has revealed the amazing plan of God. With a deeper study of scripture, she has pulled back the veil by unpacking God's Word in a practical and applicable way for all women, both married and single.

As we continually rush into the timeline of the last days, even the title of this book grips you. Susan Dunn has captured a vital link in understanding the role of both men and women working together. She captures the role of women rising to fulfill God's purpose today, as the Last Eve.

It has been my joy to know Susan for several years and to watch her grow and develop in her ministry. What she shares on the pages of this book are not theories, but they are a real-life, practical openness about her own journey of discovery. She addresses the need for single women to rise up. She also is candid about the role her husband, Derek, has played in empowering her to fulfill God's call. As a married woman, she was enabled to function and grow as a businesswoman, wife, and mother, then explode into a dynamic preacher and teacher of God's Word.

Susan's journey will resonate in your spirit as she included every aspect of life needed to become God's Last Eve. With scriptural insight and many biblical examples, she explains Eve's true role in the garden, which is a key understanding for women who have lived under the imposed guilt of the first Eve. This insight alone will liberate many women as they read this powerful book.

For such a time as this!

Reverend Dr. Naomi Dowdy
Founder Chancellor of TCA College, Singapore
Pastor, Author, Trainer, Mentor

Introduction

Ephesians 3:20

Now to Him who is able to do exceedingly abundantly above all that we ask or think, according to the power that works in us ...

If a Bible verse could sum up my journey with God, it would be Ephesians 3:20. God has taken me from a place of destruction to a promise of destiny, from a pauper to a princess, and from a near-bankrupt woman to a woman blessed with a promising business. I did not know that my life would drastically turn around when I gave myself fully into His hands.

Growing up without a father was hard. Living with a mother who had a broken heart was even harder. Rejection and a sense of abandonment were my constant companions. Survival was my only approach to life. Though I grew up attending Sunday school and hearing Bible stories, I didn't really witness His reality in my life. I tried to be a good Christian but struggled to live by faith. I was taught to love God, but trusting God was quite another matter.

Eve The Last

When I finally finished with university, I took off for the world to find a sense of worth. I was sick and tired of feeling unworthy, but I knew that feeling unworthy *and* being poor was worse. I set out to find success and climb the corporate ladder as a means of self-validation. However, after six years of searching, I found myself back in the same place called "emptiness." But this time, that place was made worse with debts that came from trying to live beyond my means to fabricate my worth.

When it seemed like all was lost, God put people in my life who brought me back to Him. At this crossroads in 1995, I decided to stop running away from God and to run toward Him. I decided to give Him my life. I didn't know then that He would give my life back to me with all that I have today. Indeed, as Ephesians 3:20 says it is above and beyond all that I could think, ask, or imagine! Back in church, I began to devour the Word and discovered my worth. The Lord divinely guided me to the financial industry, and I took a leap of faith to build a business from scratch. God truly is a debt-canceling God! In short two years, He prospered my hands and I was able to pay back all my debts to the banks! I couldn't believe that God would move so quickly, but little did I know that He was preparing me for greater things ahead.

In 1997, God showed me an open vision of the verse about the threshing floor in Luke 3:17. Immediately, I heard the Holy Spirit speak the word "preparation" into my heart. I knew God was prompting me to sign up for our Bible school in church, but I resisted. I was not intending to be a preacher, and I never thought I would end up marrying one. I was determined to be a successful businesswoman and to fund the work of the ministry. I did not respond to God's vision and ran, yet again. However, just like Jacob, God met me and gave me my ultimatum. It happened on a business-incentive trip to Milan, Italy, in September 1997. The company had paired me in the same room with another Christian lady, with whom I was chatting away as we sat on our beds, each leaning against the opposite walls. She was ranting about how good God was to her. Suddenly, I experienced the weirdest sense of déjà vu. This scene felt all so familiar, as if it had happened somehow somewhere before in my life! Yet I had never visited Milan, and I had never seen this lady before that day! Besides that, I felt deep pain as every word that came out of her mouth pierced like daggers straight into my heart. She spoke good words, but the more she said, the more I began to realize that I was lacking the favor of the Lord. Though I was a believer who faithfully tithed and served the church, He was still not Lord of all. Yes, I had decided to rededicate my life, but I had not intended to fully surrender it before that day. In that hotel room, God was ready to put His finger on that area that was yet to be on the altar.

That night, I could not sleep. Questions raced through my mind: "What is wrong with me?" "Why don't I have His favor?" My answers would come the next day. That morning, my roommate left for breakfast, and I stayed back to seek the Lord. As I prayed on my knees, God's tangible presence began to fill the room. The Holy Spirit lifted up my hands, and a voice said to me, "Susan, if I had died for you, would you live for me?" At that moment, tears flooded my eyes. I was bawling. God was exposing my fear and allowing me to see the foundation of my heart. I saw that my unwillingness to obey Him and to be trained came from my fear of letting go of security in this life—the security that came from the very thing He had placed in my hands: the success in my business. God wanted this back because He wanted to give me more. In that moment, I realized that my greatest fear was never about not being successful or rich but that I would miss out on everything I was meant to be and to do. In that wrestling experience, I allowed God to break me so that He could remake me into someone He had in mind. That day, I built an altar in my heart and became determined to live fully as He has intended—not my will but His be done.

E<small>The Last</small>ve

Now looking back, I can see that God was changing the course of my life and getting trained was pivotal to the fulfillment of the ultimate calling in my life. After graduating from Bible school, in January 1999, the Lord began to impress upon me the passage of Proverbs 31:10-31. He gave me two promises. First, my work shall be blessed, and second, that I would find my life partner, a man of spiritual authority. My business took off after I finished Bible school, and God has not stopped in the area of His provision. My business continues to grow as He continues to provide through my work for the ministry. Today, I run a financial advisory business managing more than thirty consultants and I continue to thrive in this industry. As for the life partner, well, God certainly has a sense of humor. The man turned out to be my very own pastor! Not only did I marry a pastor, but he—Derek—and I now pastor a church in Orange County, California. Derek, who left California for mission work in Malaysia in the nineties, felt called to come on staff in the church that I was a member of in Singapore. Back then, he was also my leader in our connect group.

Fast-forward: Derek and I started dating and eventually married in 2001. Over time, God began to reveal to Derek His plan to bring him back to America to start a new ministry. God also began to move in my heart to prep us for the next season. Exactly ten years later, in 2011, and with the blessings of our senior pastors, we began our journey into what we believe is our "promised land."

When I left Singapore in December 2011, I had been a volunteer pastoral leader for thirteen years. I had led 250 people and raised up leaders in what was then my home church, all while running my own financial consultancy business. The church was the largest in Singapore; it was thriving and had international influence. Every Sunday, hundreds of new converts gave their lives to Jesus; an indisputable sense of purpose and destiny surrounded the church too. Throughout my years of ministry, God had given me a heart especially for the women. Though many of them loved God deeply, they struggled with their identity and finding themselves, sometimes having to choose to be a dutiful wife or to be fervent and dedicated to the work of the ministry. It was common to see more emphasis on the spirituality of the men; oftentimes, women's spirituality was neglected, resulting likely because women are often the primary caregivers for children.

Dilemma of the Married Christian Woman

Throughout my time of ministry, I have discipled and raised up men and women leaders. In fact, Derek and I have counseled many married couples. More women than men have sought help with their issues and problems in their marriages. Marrying God-loving men who also serve the ministry has not made their issues go away. In some cases, the more "spiritual" the men become, the more the women feel a sense of disconnectedness and discontent. While their husbands are growing in their faith, the women are finding themselves in over their heads, making sure the children are taken care of and the house is clean on top of the demand of their day job! Gradually drifting away, these women begin to lose purpose and meaning and become resentful and depressed. When husbands do not intentionally encourage their wives to develop their spiritual growth together with them, it puts pressure on the marriage and threatens the degree of oneness in their relationships.

Dilemma of the Unmarried Christian Woman

Then there are the unmarried. These women (not everyone) struggle with their insecurities in their single status and constantly feel challenged to believe that they can find a soul mate. Many of them love the Lord and desire to serve Him in their calling. As women are generally maternal and great at multitasking, they make great pastoral and ministry leaders. However, they soon realize that the higher they go in their leadership position, the less likely single men in their midst are to pursue them. Their "spirituality" is now deemed to be a threat to the men and perceived as a "disadvantage" to the women. They find themselves caught in a bind—should they continue to use their gifts and serve God in the area of their passion and risk the possibility of not getting married, or should they forsake their ministry and be "palatable" to the majority of Christian men seeking a future wife?

Eventually, the women who choose the former usually end up being single for the Lord even though some really desire to be married. And the ones who choose the latter may end up married and sometimes struggle with the sense that they have become compromised in their calling.

Some women fall outside of the scenario just described. They are the few fortunate ones. The scenarios just described may also be more prevalent among Asian women than Western women because of culture and traditions; nevertheless, the latter is not totally spared of the problem.

So, how can we rationalize this? Galatians 2:20 clearly instructs us to be identified with Christ in His crucifixion and that the life we now live in the flesh we should live by faith in the Son of God. This applies to both men and women. God expects that we would live an abandoned life to the Lord whether single or married. Hence, logically speaking, we must serve the Lord in every capacity possible that would help advance the kingdom. To hold back what we can do so that we can eventually end up with somebody clearly violates the Word. In their good intent, some pastors and leaders have counseled women to hold back their ministry in order to find a spouse. I respectfully do not subscribe to this counsel for the very fact that the Bible says *"for with God all things are possible"*! If we can trust God with our salvation, can we not trust God to be our matchmaker?

Whether married or unmarried, women are created in the image and likeness of God, as are men. Together with men, they have been intentionally fashioned to be the completion of the image of God. They are made to be different and in their uniqueness to complement and not compete with men or with each other. When women do not understand God's original intent for them, they will struggle with their identity and battle with poor self-worth. On one extreme, we have women not advancing because of their lack of confidence; on the other extreme, some overcompensate for their poor self-worth by being overly aggressive and even behaving or dressing in a manly way. The Bible says that Christ has come to set us free but that freedom is not for our liberality in lifestyle but for the sole purpose to bring us back to God's original intent for us—both men and women.

With the burden to raise up women who would know the purpose of their creation and to understand their spiritual DNA, the ministry Wow31 was established. Today, Wow31 women's ministry stems from our church in Orange County with the vision to develop the W.H.O.L.E Womanhood of God to work alongside the men in our generation. Our mission is to inspire the women through the **W**ord to walk in **H**oliness with the goal to be **O**ne with our Lord Jesus. Through this oneness, the women will learn to **L**ead in their sphere of influence and **E**ngage in ministry, marketplace, and society.

In this world where men's voices primarily dominate every arena of society, the role of women in their lives is not much discussed. First, it is a highly sensitive subject; any man who dare treads into the arena knows that landmines cover it and he has very little chance to navigate through this "alive." Second, women's roles in their lives are a mystery to many men. Last but not least, it really takes a courageous man of God to look at what God has planned for him through the woman.

Eve _{The Last}

With this book, I hope to provide some answers to why enmity exists between the opposite sexes, not from a historical perspective but from what I believe is God's hidden agenda; hence, I hope to provide some fresh perspectives to managing our relationships with each other.

Before the coming back of our Lord Jesus, there will be reformation for the church, restoration in society, wealth transference in the marketplace, and most importantly, massive salvation in the harvest field. To see this come to pass, men and women must understand God's original intent for their creation, their divine mission (especially in this end-time season), and to learn to work together to defeat the works of Satan and prepare the church for the coming back of the Lord.

I pray that the Holy Spirit will give you all wisdom and understanding as you read this book. Especially, I pray that you will hear from God and know the areas in your life that He is putting His fingers on so that you can rise to the ultimate calling to be that woman He has made you to be. By doing so, you will find your message and be the oracle for God in your community.

It is so crucial to take serious note of what God would speak to you as you journey through this book because what God has hidden in creation, He is ready to highlight now!

Chapter 1

The First Eve

The Creation of Eve

An anonymous author wrote, "Sure, God created man before woman, but then again you always make a rough draft before creating the final masterpiece." We often joke about the way the first woman was created and try to make light of the somewhat subservient role that she was called to perform. Nonetheless, underneath the laughs we often question the meaning of our existence and struggle to think that we were created just to be helpers to men.

I was one of those who just couldn't wrap my head around the fact that God, who is our fair judge, would create us beneath men! To think that we are only an extension of man's rib! I found it preposterous to fathom that my whole reason for existence is to help men or a man! Can you relate? I know that many women struggle with this.

The creation of mankind has intrigued many and raised questions about the way and the order that we were created. How could a God who loved the world so much set an order where one of His creations rules over another?

Eve The Last

Genesis 2:18-20

And the Lord God said, "It is not good that man should be alone; I will make him a helper comparable to him." Out of the ground the Lord God formed every beast of the field and every bird of the air, and brought them to Adam to see what he would call them. And whatever Adam called each living creature, that was its name. So Adam gave names to all cattle, to the birds of the air, and to every beast of the field. But for Adam there was not found a helper comparable to him.

An initial reading of this Bible passage provides an erroneous impression that God was looking for a "helper" amongst the animals. In verse 18, God observed that it was not good for Adam to be alone and saw that he needed a helper. The next event we read about is God and Adam having a day at the zoo!

God seems to have overlooked something. Did it just finally occur to Him that Adam needed a helper and not a single animal was good enough to fit the bill? Of course, we know the answer is *NO!* Our God, who knows all things from the beginning to the end and the end to the beginning, makes no mistakes. He is our master builder. We can trust Him. So, what point did God want to make? Psalm 147:5 says, *"Great is our Lord, and mighty in power; His understanding is infinite."* As much as it appears to be, Eve was never an afterthought for God. Adam and Eve existed in God's mind before creation, and may I persuade you that Eve was created at the same time as Adam, except she was purposefully hidden until the right time for her to be revealed to Adam.

Woman Hidden in Creation and Revealed on Purpose

Genesis 1:26-27

Then God said, "Let Us make man in Our image, according to Our likeness; let them have dominion over the fish of the sea, over the birds of the air, and over the cattle, over all the earth and over every creeping thing that creeps on the earth." So God created man in His own image; in the image of God He created him (Adam); male and female He created them.

In this passage, we see that God has created man in His image and with His likeness and that Adam contained the male and female likeness or attributes of God. At the beginning of Adam's creation, Eve was hidden in him. God then, with full intention, took Eve out from Adam, but not without first taking Adam to the zoo. I sometimes find myself chuckling whenever I think about this. God always intended for man to find his life partner in a woman, but many today find companionship in their pets instead. I'm sure you've seen what looked like a beautiful baby stroller, peered in, and saw a dog instead!

To desire safe companionship, often we have veered far from God's central thought and intention about life and relationships. In this intriguing manner of creation, God wanted us to understand certain divine concepts. Romans 1:20 says, *"For since the creation of the world His invisible attributes are clearly seen, being understood by the things that are made, even His eternal power and Godhead, so that they are without excuse."* We must understand that our God is a great teacher and to understand His infinite ways and wisdom, He needs to demonstrate and inspire us to come to this conclusion ourselves. As it is said, "The mediocre teacher talks. The good teacher explains. The superior teacher demonstrates. The great teacher inspires!" So, what was God trying to illustrate through the way humankind was created and the way Eve arrived on the scene? What does our Great Teacher want to reveal to us? Here lies the key to becoming the Last Eve he intended for us to be as women.

Demonstrating the Relationship between Christ and the Church

Our Omniscient God, knowing the end from the beginning, had a plan of redemption for the world that He loves: to give us Jesus, and through Him the church will be birthed so that she can be the answer for the world. God formed the woman from the side of man. Likewise, the church came from the side of Christ. This is a beautiful type and shadow.

Eve was formed from Adam's substance; she was of human substance yet formed differently and was what Adam was not. She was the finishing touch and completion of God's creation of mankind.

In creation, God shows us that man and woman must be one to carry the full image and complete the likeness of God. When the church is one with Jesus, only then can we bring righteousness to our world. This provides a beautiful symbolism of when a man and a woman fully embrace their own design and work together in agreement and harmony. Whether in a marriage or otherwise, they provide a complete image of God for the whole world to see!

God created the first Adam with Eve hidden on the inside and declared that together they are the image and the likeness of Him! So, in creation, God divided one into two, but in a marriage, the two must come back to being one!

Demonstrating the Relationship between Husband and Wife in a Marriage

This understanding helps us know the purpose of God in a relationship between a husband and a wife in marriage. In Genesis 2, the Lord God put Adam into a deep sleep, and while he slept, God took one of Adam's ribs (really? let's come back to this shortly) and fashioned it into a woman. God brought her to Adam, from which Adam exclaimed she was "now bone of my bones and flesh of my flesh." Adam called her woman because she was taken out of man. At this point, God established the concept of marriage, husband and wife, and leaving and cleaving.

Genesis 2:24

Therefore a man shall leave his father and mother and be joined to his wife, and they shall become one flesh.

God divided woman from man so that each would seek out the other and become one to complete and reflect the full glory of God, just like how Jesus fully adopted the church as His bride. Gary Thomas, in his book *Sacred Marriage*, said, "The Church is the bride of Christ, the new Adam's new Eve. She was prefigured in creation, prepared for in the Old Testament and announced by John the Baptist, founded by Christ, fulfilled by His cross and resurrection, and has been empowered with the filling of the Holy Spirit."

His wife must be his most sought-after disciple.

Ephesians clarified further and gave details about how this oneness can be achieved:

Ephesians 5:22-33 (NIV)

Wives, submit yourselves to your own husbands as you do to the Lord. For the husband is the head of the wife as Christ is the head of the church, his body, of which he is the Savior. Now as the church submits to Christ, so also wives should submit to their husbands in everything. Husbands, love your wives, just as Christ loved the church and gave himself up for her to make her holy, cleansing her by the washing with water through the word, and to present her to himself as a radiant church, without stain or wrinkle or any other blemish, but holy and blameless. In this same way, husbands ought to love their wives as their own bodies. He who loves his wife loves himself. After all, no one ever hated their own body, but they feed and care for their body, just as Christ does the church—for we are members of his body. "For this reason a man will leave his father and mother and be united to his wife, and the two will become one flesh." This is a profound mystery—but I am talking about Christ and the church. However, each one of you also must love his wife as he loves himself, and the wife must respect her husband.

Ephesians 5 gives us a recipe for creating oneness in marriage. Yes, it is possible! The common thread throughout the passage is to see and treat our spouses as ourselves. The man is commanded to love his wife as himself and to follow Christ's example "to make her holy, cleansing her by the washing with water through the Word." Beyond the flowers and the date nights, God expects man to nurture woman by the constant reminding, teaching, and sharing of the Word of the Lord with her. *His wife must be his most sought-after disciple.* However, in my many years of ministry, I have not seen many men willingly disciple their wives or teach them or nurture them to come to the fullness of who they are meant to be. In my opinion, one of the best ways a man can create a sense of great worth in a woman is to teach and nurture her through the Word. This empowers and frees a woman in her identity in God and role in a marriage. I understand that some men may feel ill-equipped to do so or maybe they have tried but didn't get the result they were seeking (we will touch on this again later in the book). Jesus did that when He was on this Earth, making sure to acknowledge women, publicly admonish them, and teach them the ways of the kingdom. Many women who followed Him became effective colaborers with the men for the widespread spreading of the gospel.

In reality, many times women are more passionate about spiritual things and more actively involved in the ministry of the church. Women seem to be the person in the marriage who is more concerned about their young adopting the faith. In fact, many times wives decide where the family will establish their spiritual home. On the other hand, generally their husbands couldn't care less about where they attend church as long as their wives are happy. They do not talk or discuss much about the Word in their homes and much less so with their wives. Meanwhile, men who are pursuing God and serving in the ministry tend to preach more to their congregation than share the Word at home. They spend much more time mentoring their flock but miss out on discipling the one who is the most important: their wife.

Women need to be discipled, whether in their marriage, business, ministry, or otherwise. Men must see our worth and understand our value because of this fact: We exist for the men in our generation.

Woman Was Made for Man

1 Corinthians 11:8-9

For man is not from woman, but woman from man. Nor was man created for the woman, but woman for the man.

Again, God plainly and without apology lays it out for both men and women to understand that woman was made for man ultimately because the church is made for Christ. Though in today's *me-centered* theology, many believe and behave as if Christ exists for them, the believer, yet that could not be further from the truth! Hence, in the same way, woman was for the purpose of man and what he needs to receive from her to fully come to his destiny! May I also say that in doing so, the woman likewise can fulfill the primary role she was created for. Let's revisit Genesis 2.

Genesis 2:18

And the Lord God said, "It is not good that man should be alone; I will make him a helper comparable to him."

Eve The Last

God's original intent for woman was that she would help the man; this is not restricted to the context of marriage. However, within a marriage and more so in a family, the role of the woman being a helper is even more pronounced.

If you are a woman, how do you feel knowing that you are made for man? Before you get provoked, may I persuade you that this call to be a helper does not denote one of less importance or inferiority. First, let me kindly refute the notion that Eve was created out of a rib taken from Adam's side.

Just for laughs …

Adam was walking around the Garden of Eden feeling very lonely, so God asked him,

"What is wrong with you?"

Adam said he didn't have anyone to talk to.

God said he was going to give him a companion: a woman.

God said this person would cook for him, wash his clothes, and agree with all of his decisions.

She would bear his children and never ask him to get up in the middle of the night to take care of them.

She would not nag him and would always be the first to admit she was wrong when they had a disagreement.

She would never have a headache and would freely give him love and compassion whenever needed.

"But, Adam, this is going to cost you," God said.

"How much will this WOMAN cost me, Lord?" Adam replied.

God answered, "An arm and a leg."

Adam pondered this for some time. Then with a look of deep thought and concern still etched on his face, he said, "Eh, what can I get for just a rib?

Well, we all know if you pay peanuts, you get monkeys! And women are not monkeys (although we may act like them sometimes when we don't get our way). We are made from more than a piece of rib!

All of us have learned from the Bible that God created woman from a rib taken out of Adam. I accepted this without question until a few years ago when the Holy Spirit started to prompt questions in my heart to seek the truth about the purpose and role of women spiritually, in the kingdom, and in society. While searching for the answers, I began to realize that not only was she created from more than a rib, Eve was fashioned with great substance. In her design, God mysteriously wired her to be what Adam was not and to do what Adam could not. Men, on their own, can do great things, but when women come alongside them, they will achieve greater heights. Woman is like the wind beneath his wings, the arrows in his hands; she holds the key to unlock greatness in his life.

> **Woman is like the wind beneath his wings, the arrows in his hands; she holds the key to unlock greatness in his life.**

Genesis 2:21-22

*And the Lord God caused a deep sleep to fall on Adam, and he slept; and He took one of his ribs and closed up the flesh in its place. Then the **rib** which the Lord God had taken from man He made into a woman, and He brought her to the man.*

The original Hebrew word used here, which the Bible translates as *rib*, is *"tslea."* Nowhere else in the Bible is this word translated as *rib*. The other forty-one times it is used in its original form or variation, it is translated as *side*.

Some examples:

- Exodus 37   It refers to the sides of the Ark of the Covenant.

- Exodus 27   It refers to "the two sides of the altar."

- Exodus 26   It refers to "the side of the tabernacle."

- I Kings 6   It refers to the two identical sides or panels of the folding doors of Solomon's temple.

- Job 18   Job refers to "calamities at his side."

- Jeremiah 20   Jeremiah speaks of "fear on every side."

Discovering what you are designed to do will give you a road map to develop yourself.

God formed woman from material taken from the side of man. A rib had nothing to do with it. In fact, God literally divided Adam into half and created Eve from material from his side. Even today, people sometimes refer to their spouse as their other half or their better half, and that somehow seems appropriate.

Adam's response now takes on new significance when he says in Genesis 2:23, *"This is now bone of my bones and flesh of my flesh; she shall be called Woman, because she was taken out of Man."*

In creation, God divided one into two but …

In marriage, the two must become one again …

Knowing that you have been intricately fashioned to be a helper to men should not make you feel "less than" about yourself. In fact, it should intrigue you to discover exactly how you are to help them. Discovering what you are designed to do will give you a road map to develop yourself. You are not constantly fighting to be noticed for the wrong reason. In the last decade, many women's ministries have come into existence and every year women's conferences are held all throughout the world. Most of these conferences inevitably address the identity of women and seek to affirm them. Without understanding our God-given design, I believe our identities are incomplete and our confidence as women has no solid foundation.

> **Without understanding our God-given design, I believe our identities are incomplete and our confidence as women has no solid foundation.**

Beyond our natural and physical roles, women play an important spiritual role in men's lives, especially so in this end-time dispensation. As I begin to unfold some of these spiritual roles, my deepest desire is for you to fully comprehend the heart of the Father who fashioned you and for you to embrace your true worth, becoming all that you are designed to be and fulfilling all that you are called to do.

Eve was fearfully and wonderfully made. God made her with great intentions. Such intentions were hidden in the beginning, but heaven is ready to highlight what she was made of and how she, together with Adam, will bring God's dominion to the earth. Every woman after Eve represents an extension of her. As women evolve throughout time, they will come to the full understanding of their role in the end-times. I believe the time is now! What God has hidden in creation, heaven is ready to highlight the special design of her creation and her end-time

E The Last ve

assignment. I pray that God will bring revelation, healing, and courage as you journey with me through this book. Woman, you are wonderfully and beautifully made!

Chapter 2

The Gift

In delaying the creation of Eve, God gave Adam a lesson in the basic pattern and design of how humanity is to bear God's own image and bring Him glory: as man and woman. Now, Adam and Eve, together, complete this wondrous monument to God's image. Eve was made to join Adam in loving God and to help him bring God glory.

By distinctively separating the creation of Adam and Eve, I believe God was drawing Adam's attention to the *gift of Eve*. Recently, a friend's family surprised him on his birthday, waking him up by bursting into his room, shouting, "Surprise!" I imagine God doing the same with Adam; he was fast asleep when God divided his flesh and formed the woman out of his body. Adam didn't ask for a companion because he didn't think he needed one. But God, in all His wisdom, knew that it was not good for Adam to be alone. God surprised Adam with someone who was like him yet fashioned so differently. She was beautiful to behold, colorful in her emotions, soft to the touch yet strong in her spirit.

Genesis 2:18

Then the Lord God said, "It is not good that man should be alone. I will make him a helper suitable for him."

Eve The Last

Some men may argue that woman is not a gift based on what happened after Eve came forth. The prelude to the fall of mankind was her desire to partake of the fruit from the tree of the knowledge of good and evil, which God specifically forbade. Until today, many women are still judged and forbidden to preach or teach in church because of what happened in the Garden of Eden. I ask this: Did God not know this would happen before Eve was brought forth? Nonetheless, Eve's actions did not negate the fact that God intended for her to be a gift to the man. You see, beyond the outward things that a woman can do, what's embedded within her needs to be uncovered and nurtured so that it will be a blessing to whom she is sent. In this chapter, I want to talk about Eve's desire for wisdom and how it is God's intention for her to be a display of His wisdom on Earth.

In times past, many preachers have taught that Eve took the forbidden fruit because of mankind's inherent desire to operate independently of God. It was Adam who instructed her regarding the fruit. As the instruction came from Adam and not from God directly, Eve's sin would be her insubordination to the man directly and God indirectly; Adam was an implied authority of God over her life.

What intrigues me more is why the devil tempted Eve and not Adam and why she was tempted. Eve was not lusting after the fruit because of how delicious it would taste; she desired it because of what it would give her: the ability to discern between good and evil, which is wisdom.

Does God not want Adam and Eve—and every one of us—to know the difference between good and evil? Is desiring wisdom a rebellion against God?

Proverbs 4:7

Wisdom is the principal thing;
Therefore, get wisdom.
And in all your getting, get understanding.

God wants us to know the difference between good and evil, and He especially wired into woman the desire for the knowledge of it. Have you ever noticed that most women's ministries name themselves after some form of wisdom and that this is not same with men's ministries? It's not that men are not wise nor desire to be wise; it's just that women have been designed to activate more prominently in wisdom. And the devil knows it too. So, before Eve could fully develop her gift, the devil tempted her to break her covenant with Adam through her disobedience.

> **When we step out from His order, we are literally opening the door for demons to infiltrate our territory!**

Eve's original sin was her insubordination to Adam. What was Adam's? The Bible says he was not deceived, but his sin was his reluctance to protect and lead Eve. So, when the man refused to lead and nurture, and the woman refused to submit and be led, the world plunged into chaos and both Adam and Eve lost their earthly dominion. The Bible says the keys to this world were now given to Satan. God's order brings about the blessings of God. On the other hand, when we step out from His order, we are literally opening the door for demons to infiltrate our territory!

But God!

God sent Jesus (the Second Adam), who would commit to His order. He was sent to die for this world so that through His death, the keys of dominion would be taken back and God's order would be reestablished. Jesus's sacrifice demonstrated to man how he can lay down his life to fight for his bride. Jesus's obedience showed the woman how she should submit to her husband just as He submitted to the Father. His death reconciled the body to the head and the woman to the man.

Man and woman, surrendered to God, must now come in agreement to operate in God's order so that the powers of darkness are kept out and God's blessings will manifest in society.

As a woman of God, our obedience is first to our Lord Jesus Christ. Then from this alignment we will have grace to submit to man despite the difficulties and the inconveniences. Without a complete surrender to God, it will be hard to submit and impossible to fulfill our roles to be that gift to the men of our generation. Our God is a good-giver, and He gives regardless of how undeserving the receiver. He gives His all. He gives His best.

Eve Was the Most Extravagant Gift

God gave His Son, Jesus, the most extravagant gift He could bestow upon us. He was fully assured that this gift would be the perfect answer to the world. He knew, without a shadow of a doubt, that Jesus would accomplish His assignment. Likewise, Eve was an extravagant gift to Adam.

James 1:17

Every good gift and every perfect gift is from above, and comes down from the Father of lights, with whom there is no variation or shadow of turning.

Our Omnipotent Father knows all things. He doesn't make a mistake. You are never a mistake no matter the circumstances you were born into. You came from God even before you were formed in your mother's womb.

Jeremiah 1:5

Before I formed you in the womb, I knew you;
Before you were born, I sanctified you;
I ordained you a prophet to the nations.

Everyone thought that Ishmael was a mistake. His mother, Hagar, was forced to have a child with her master, Abraham, because his wife, Sarah, was tired of waiting for God's promise of a son. However, Ishmael was not the son that God promised to give to Sarah, but God knew he would be born. God blessed him anyway, despite the circumstances of his birth.

He has hidden in the beginning the full mystery of her design, as she has a very important assignment in the end-times dispensation.

Genesis 16:11

And the Angel of the Lord said to her:
"Behold, you are with child,
And you shall bear a son.
You shall call his name Ishmael..."

You are a gift that God has especially prepared for this world. He has sent you to your family and your generation to be a blessing and to bring about change so that blessings can continue to flow into the lives of the people connected to you. You were not born at any other time because you were born for such a time as now—to make your mark and be a gift to the people that God has given you.

E^{The Last}ve

Jesus was the most extravagant gift to this world. God gave Him because the world needed Him, though the world did not fully comprehend that when He was given. The world could not comprehend the fullness of what He was supposed to do. In the same way, I believe that the world did not fully comprehend the full intent of God for women. Hence, she had been much confined to her natural roles and duties. I am fully convinced that this is God's intentional doing. He has hidden in the beginning the full mystery of her design, as she has a very important assignment in the end-times dispensation. At this point, God is ready to highlight what is hidden. Heaven is progressively revealing the specific design of women, and we are now discovering our ultimate assignment in this end-time. You will discover what that is as you journey through this book.

How can we as women be an extravagant gift? To begin, we must be prepared to give ourselves fully to what God has ordained our lives to be—just like Paul, who, in his valedictory speech near the end of his life, likened himself to be like a drink fully poured out. As Jesus did, we also should purpose to fulfill our destiny and declare at the end of our lives, "It is finished!"

You may not be in the best place right now or feel that you are impacting people and society in the manner that you have dreamed. You must understand that Jesus did not fulfill His destiny in the world the same day He was born; he had to evolve into the person that would manifest His God-given gift in the way the Father intended.

Eve did not seem to have a strong start, and we know little about her except what we read about her time in the Garden of Eden. However, her story has continued in the lives of every woman succeeding her in the Bible and the women of every generation to follow. This narrative of the woman is evolving, and I believe we are seeing the final chapters of her full development and her glorious destiny in this end-time.

Eve Was the Evolving Gift

When Jesus was twelve years old, His earthly parents lost Him in Jerusalem during the Feast of the Passover. They found Him, after three days, in the temple, sitting in the midst of the teachers. His mother questioned Him, and He replied, "Why did you seek Me? Did you not know that I must be about My Father's business?" God did not give Jesus instant understanding, power, or the grace to be the Savior of the world. Jesus had to learn and grow to know His Heavenly Father and fully grasp His destiny through revelation. Not only that, He had to learn to submit to the earthly authorities that God had ordained for Him. Through His hunger for the things of heaven and His submission to the authority of this world, He grew in wisdom, stature, and in favor with God and men.

Luke 2:51-52

Then He went down with them and came to Nazareth, and was subject to them, but His mother kept all these things in her heart. And Jesus increased in wisdom and stature, and in favor with God and men.

Will you, likewise, have the same posture and hunger after the things of heaven? Will you fully submit to the Lord? Will you give yourself fully to pursue this relationship you have with the Father? When you do so, you will begin to see the difficulties of your situation in a different light. You will find the grace to obey the Word of the Bible. You will have strength to overcome the emotions and break the defeating mindsets that come to keep you in the pit. Helen Keller said, "When we do the best we can, we never know what miracle is wrought in our life, or in the life of another." Purpose each day and all times to be the best version of yourself, not for the admiration of others but for the applause of the One who matters the most.

Eve The Last

Philippians 3:2

Not that I have already attained, or am already perfected; but I press on, that I may lay hold of that for which Christ Jesus has also laid hold of me.

I greatly admire apostle Paul's hunger for God and his holy determination to have all that God intended for him. Paul did not fear acknowledging his imperfection. Matthew Henry, in his commentary, mentioned, "The best men in the world will readily own their imperfection in the present state." May I say the same for us women—we must never shy away to acknowledge our imperfection; instead, we must continue to *press on* and *pursue* with vigor, as we pursue the high call of Christ in our lives. We must endeavor to get more grace, do more good, and to never think we have done enough. Our standing is not in our perfection but in the righteousness of Christ and not trying to prove ourselves. In doing this, God will unpack everything He has placed on the inside of us.

> **God uses our sufferings to bring the hidden things within us to a place of visibility.**

Eleanor Roosevelt was accurate to say, "A woman is like a tea bag—you never know how strong she is until she gets in hot water." In my many years of ministering, I have seen countless women overcome great adversities and sorrows; because of what they overcame, they are a powerful source of hope and help to their families and their communities.

2 Corinthians 4:7-10

But we have this treasure in earthen vessels, that the excellence of the power may be of God and not of us. We are hard-pressed on every side, yet not crushed; we are perplexed, but not in despair; persecuted, but not forsaken;

struck down, but not destroyed—always carrying about in the body the dying of the Lord Jesus, that the life of Jesus also may be manifested in our body.

Suffering is part and parcel of the result of our broken-down world. Instead of shielding us from this world, God uses our sufferings to bring the hidden things within us to a place of visibility. Truth to be told, if we yield to God while going through the fire, we would truly see the precious pearl within. Consider how a pearl forms in an oyster: It occurs when an object somehow enters the oyster, and instead of ejecting the object, as most humans would try to do, the oyster secretes a multilayered substance to cover it. The object that came in as an irritant has turned into something lovely within the life of the oyster. And still the Bible says we are more precious than pearls!

Proverbs 31:10 (AMP)

An excellent woman [one who is spiritual, capable, intelligent, and virtuous], who is he who can find her? Her value is more precious than jewels and her worth is far above rubies or pearls.

In the realm of the spirit world, we existed as spiritual beings before we became physical beings. We were then dispatched from heaven to fulfill God's purpose for our generation. When we are born into this world, we come through a process, a series of continuous actions, changes, and steps to achieve a purpose and destiny. According to apostle Mike Connell of Ascend Global Church, the *law of process* is God's ordained way to complete and fulfill your purpose. The higher the call, the stronger the process. To fulfill your purpose, you must go through the law of process. One ultimate purpose exists—to be transformed into Christ's likeness—but many processes exist in life. The process changes you. Its main role is to qualify each of us for our purpose and give us the power to fulfill it. Unfortunately, the law of process is not an option; it is necessary if we truly want to discover what God has gifted us for and how our gift will benefit this world. Fortunately, God promises us that we will not be tested beyond what we can bear.

1 Corinthians 10:13 (TPT)

We all experience times of testing, which is normal for every human being. But God will be faithful to you. He will screen and filter the severity, nature, and timing of every test or trial you face so that you can bear it. And each test is an opportunity to trust him more, for along with every trial God has provided for you a way of escape that will bring you out of it victoriously.

After understanding the law of process, we then can face challenges with perseverance and understand the expectations that come at the end: victory, wisdom, and power. You must know that God will never leave you to go through the fire alone. He promises to never leave you nor forsake you.

The Story of the Refiner (Author Unknown)

A group of women were studying the book of Malachi in the Old Testament. They read chapter three, verse three: *"He will sit as a refiner and purifier of silver."* This verse puzzled the women. They wondered what this statement meant about the character and nature of God. One of the women offered to find out about the process of refining silver and get back to the group at their next Bible study.

That week, this woman made an appointment with a silversmith to watch him at work. She did not mention anything about the reason for her interest beyond her curiosity about the process of refining silver. As she watched the silversmith, he held a piece of silver over the fire and let it heat up. He explained that in refining silver, one needs to hold the silver in the middle of the fire; that's where the flames are hottest so they burn away all the impurities.

The woman thought about God holding us in such a hot spot; then she thought again about the verse, that he sits as a refiner and purifier of silver. She asked the silversmith if it was true that he had to sit in front of the fire the whole time he was refining the silver.

The man answered "yes" and explained that not only did he have to do that but he had to keep his eyes on the silver the entire time. If the silver was left even a moment too long in the flames, it would be damaged.

For a moment, the woman sat in silence. Then she asked, "How do you know when the silver is fully refined?"

He smiled at her and answered, "Oh, that's easy—when I see my image in it."

The ultimate aim of the law of process is to develop the person of Jesus on the inside of us. With that, we become the right candidate to receive the power, wisdom, and creativity to fulfill our purpose.

Malachi 3:2-3

"But who can endure the day of His coming? And who can stand when He appears? For He is like a refiner's fire and like launderers' soap. He will sit as a refiner and a purifier of silver; He will purify the sons of Levi, and purge them as gold and silver, that they may offer to the Lord an offering in righteousness."

"That they may offer to the Lord an offering in righteousness"— would you yield yourself to God while going through the process and continue to let His Spirit mold you into the kind of gift (to the men and everyone else in your generation) that He has always imagined you to be?

E^{The Last}ve

Eve Was the Encompassing Gift

Paul, in 2 Corinthians 9:15, described Jesus as the "indescribable gift," and indeed this is so true! The gift of Jesus is multidimensional. Through Him we can access our inheritance in heaven and dominance here on Earth. Heaven is now accessible to us through His blood, and Earth is under our feet through His resurrection. Beyond that, embedded within Jesus is the gift of the Holy Spirit. Matthew recorded John the Baptist saying, "I indeed baptize you with water unto repentance, but He who is coming after me is mightier than I, whose sandals I am not worthy to carry. He will baptize you with the Holy Spirit and fire" (Matt. 3:11). Let's see what John says regarding the Holy Spirit.

John 7:38-40

"He who believes in Me, as the Scripture has said, out of his heart will flow rivers of living water." But this He spoke concerning the Spirit, whom those believing in Him would receive; for the Holy Spirit was not yet given, because Jesus was not yet glorified.

It is crystal clear that the Holy Spirit is the gift within the gift of Jesus Christ. One cannot receive the Holy Spirit without first receiving the Lord. The Holy Spirit is the promise of the Father given to our Lord. This promise came with a condition that Jesus Christ would lay down His life for all of us. What an incredible sacrifice! For the Father to promise the Holy Spirit to come on all flesh, if the flesh so wills, we must know then that the Holy Spirit plays an indispensable role in our heavenly inheritance and earthly dominance. So, who is the Person of the Holy Spirit? What kind of gift is He?

Romans 8:15 described the Holy Spirit as the Spirit that births our adoption process into the kingdom. Through Him, we can be grafted into sonship. Through Him, we can know the love (Rom. 5:5) that our

Father has for us, so much so that we can call Him our *"Abba"* (Daddy). Romans 15:13 further ascribes the ability for the believer to receive joy, peace, and hope through the Holy Spirit who dwells within us. Along with this power comes the activation of the believer to be an effective witness in their communities of the reality of God.

Acts 1:8

But you shall receive power when the Holy Spirit comes upon you. And you shall be My witnesses in Jerusalem, and in all Judea and Samaria, and to the ends of the earth.

Additional spiritual gifts dwell within the gift of the Holy Spirit. Along with the Person of the Holy Spirit, God distributes to each one of us various gifts to bring about continuous spiritual renewal in the body.

1 Corinthians 12:4-11

There are diversities of gifts, but the same Spirit. There are differences of ministries, but the same Lord. And there are diversities of activities, but it is the same God who works all in all. But the manifestation of the Spirit is given to each one for the profit of all: for to one is given the word of wisdom through the Spirit, to another the word of knowledge through the same Spirit, to another faith by the same Spirit, to another gifts of healings by the same Spirit, to another the working of miracles, to another prophecy, to another discerning of spirits, to another different kinds of tongues, to another the interpretation of tongues. But one and the same Spirit works all these things, distributing to each one individually as He wills.

Her spiritual capability is like a deep well and is waiting to be discovered.

Eve The Last

The gift of Eve and all that she can do, like the Holy Spirit, comes in multiple dimensions. Beyond her natural abilities and earthly functions, her spiritual capability is like a deep well and is waiting to be discovered. This is true for all women, and when they are awakened, and wholly healed and alive, we will see great movement in the territory they have been gifted. God knows what He put on the inside of women; the devil knows what women are capable of doing. Do you know?

God intended Eve to be more than Adam's companion, but her role was never really expounded upon in the Bible. I believe this was done with all intention because women's ultimate assignment, beyond the natural roles and duties, has very much to do with the final battle between Satan and the church. Women are to work with men to establish the power of God's kingdom. However, first she has to evolve and come to the place of full revelation of the gift she is meant to be.

Chapter 3

She Is a Warrior

I read a story on the internet that so moved me. I refer to it often as a remarkable example of a woman who will risk her life to fight for another person's life. It is a story of a woman who knows the pain of considering an abortion. Her name is Pam. Let's read her story ...

"More than 24 years ago, she and her husband Bob were serving as missionaries to the Philippines and praying for a fifth child. Pam contracted amoebic dysentery, an infection of the intestine caused by a parasite found in contaminated food or drink. She went into a coma and was treated with strong antibiotics before they discovered she was pregnant.

"Doctors urged her to abort the baby for her own safety and told her that the medicines had caused irreversible damage to her baby. She refused the abortion and cited her Christian faith as the reason for her hope that her son would be born without the devastating disabilities physicians predicted. Pam said the doctors didn't think of it as a life, they thought of it as a mass of fetal tissue.

"While pregnant, Pam nearly lost their baby four times but refused to consider abortion. She recalled making a pledge to God with her husband: 'If you will give us a son, we'll name him Timothy and we'll make him a preacher.'

"Pam ultimately spent the last two months of her pregnancy in bed and eventually gave birth to a healthy baby boy August 14, 1987. Pam's youngest son is indeed a preacher. He preaches in prisons, makes hospital visits, and serves with his father's ministry in the Philippines. He also plays football. Pam's son is Tim Tebow.

"The University of Florida's star quarterback became the first sophomore in history to win college football's highest award, the Heisman Trophy.

"Tebow kneeling in prayer, which has since been referred to as 'Tebowing,' was recognized as a word in the English language by the Global Language Monitor, due to its level of worldwide usage.

"Tebow is known for his outspoken Christian faith. In the Philippines, Tim Tebow preached to schools and villages, and assisted in medical care. Tebow supports more than 40 national evangelists working in that nation. In the United States, he has shared his Christian faith in prisons and schools, to church and youth groups, and at meetings and conferences. Tebow holds a firm stance in favor of faith-based abstinence and has maintained his virginity until marriage.

"An Easter Sunday crowd of roughly 20,000 in Florida listened to Tebow on April 8, 2012. Tebow said, 'Regardless of what happens, I still honor my Lord and Savior Jesus Christ, because at the end of the day, that's what's important, win or lose. … We need to get back to one nation under God, and be role models for kids,' Tebow added."

What an incredible young man! However, he would not be if his mom hadn't fought for his life! Women are warriors. They will fight for the ones they love—their husbands, children, and for people they do not know, such as the disadvantaged and the disabled; some fight for world causes such as climate change and social justice. Despite the hardness of life, women always find a way to survive and many even thrive. Men are created to be strong and visionaries, but women are created to fight alongside men to establish the kingdom of God on this earth before the Lord returns.

After God created Adam, who is the complete likeness and image of Himself, He declared His satisfaction in what He had made and declared that it was very good! Yet a little further, in the next chapter, it appeared as if God realized that something was amiss and that Adam, by himself, was incomplete.

Of course, we understand that God does not make mistakes and that He has, all the while, intended humankind to be of two sexes: man and woman. He intends for the man and woman to come together and be fruitful, to reproduce, and fill the earth. God is relational, and He loves to fellowship. He has fellowship amongst the Holy Trinity: God the Father, the Son, and the Holy Spirit, and He wants to replicate the same kind of relationship with people. This includes you! So, exactly what kind of relationship does He want us to have with Him?

If we examine the kind of relationship that God has within the Holy Trinity, we will understand the kind of relationship He wants to see among us. Though God the Father is the headship, He chose to operate His sovereign will on this earth through His Son. John 1:3 says, *"All things were made through Jesus and without Him nothing was made that was made."* The Father granted for His Son to carry His glory and fully reflect His power. He is not insecure and definitely not territorial. The Son, on the other hand, knowing fully the power given to Him, did not choose to operate independently of the Father. Take a look at what He says here:

Eve The Last

Then Jesus answered and said to them, "Most assuredly, I say to you, the Son can do nothing of Himself, but what He sees the Father do; for whatever He does, the Son also does in like manner. For the Father loves the Son and shows Him all things that He Himself does; and He will show Him greater works than these, that you may marvel."

What a beautiful relationship the Father and Son have. What about the Holy Spirit's role? The Bible tells us that the Holy Spirit is the promise from the Father given to our Lord Jesus on the condition that Jesus would die for the sin of this world. Jesus testifies that this Helper is sent by Him from the Father (John 15:26). The Holy Spirit, who is the full embodiment of God in spirit form, receives instruction from Jesus, and the Holy Spirit's main purpose is not to highlight Himself but to testify of the Son. The Holy Spirit also is assigned to glorify Jesus and take what belongs to Jesus and declare it to us.

John 16:13-14

However, when He, the Spirit of truth, has come, He will guide you into all truth; for He will not speak on His own authority, but whatever He hears He will speak; and He will tell you things to come. He will glorify Me, for He will take of what is Mine and declare it to you.

Before you start thinking that the Holy Spirit is the least of the Holy Trinity, think again! The Holy Spirit is assigned to fully serve God, and for this reason, God (the Father) highly regards the Holy Spirit. He has no physical form. He does not speak on His own authority. He lives to highlight the Son. Because of all of this, the Father ensures that the Holy Spirit is not disregarded; on the contrary, He is highly honored.

Matthew 12:31-33

Therefore I say to you, every sin and blasphemy will be forgiven men, but the blasphemy against the Spirit will not be forgiven men. Anyone who speaks a word against the Son of Man, it will be forgiven him; but whoever speaks against the Holy Spirit, it will not be forgiven him, either in this age or in the age to come.

Wow! The Father ensures that no person disregards the One who is unseen and mandated to be the Helper to us all.

So, this is the kind of relationship that the Father wanted for Adam and Eve—one in which they are interdependent with each other, submitting to each other in reverence, and fighting for one another in love. Ephesians 5 summarizes the command for us to *"submit to one another in the fear of God."* Through Paul's letter to the Ephesian church, God began to expound on this kind of relationship and how it relates to the relationship between Christ and the church.

Ephesians 5:22-33

Wives, submit to your own husbands, as to the Lord. For the husband is head of the wife, as also Christ is head of the church; and He is the Savior of the body. Therefore, just as the church is subject to Christ, so let the wives be to their own husbands in everything. Husbands, love your wives, just as Christ also loved the church and gave Himself for her, that He might sanctify and cleanse her with the washing of water by the word, that He might present her to Himself a glorious church, not having spot or wrinkle or any such thing, but that she should be holy and without blemish. So husbands ought to love their own wives as their own bodies; he who loves his wife loves himself. For no one ever hated his own flesh, but nourishes and cherishes it, just as the Lord does the church. For we are members of His body, of His flesh and of His bones. "For this reason a man shall leave his father and mother and be joined to his wife, and the two shall become one flesh." This is a great mystery, but I speak concerning Christ and the church. Nevertheless let each one of you in particular so love his own wife as himself, and let the wife see that she respects her husband.

Clearly, God wanted the man and woman to fight for each other. Both fight differently because they are designed differently. Although women are the "weaker vessel," God made them to be a significant help to men. The original Hebrew words used for the word *"helper"* or *"help meet"* are ***"ezer kenegdo."***

Let us first touch on the word "kenegdo." The Hebrew word kenegdo means opposite as to him or corresponding as to him—similar in nature yet different. A woman is not better or less than the man. Man and woman are equally and uniquely created, a perfect fit.

Ezer has two original meanings in Hebrew, which are: to rescue/ save and to be strong. In the Old Testament, *ezer* appears twenty-one times. This helper that God gave to Adam was meant to be more than a hand-holder but rather a significant, substantial presence. The same word *ezer* was used in Ezekiel 12, Daniel 11, and Isaiah 30, referring to military aid, the kind of a protection from armed forces, while Exodus 18, Deuteronomy 33, and Hosea 13 indicated an even more powerful help from God Himself. Is God trying to tell us something here? Beyond our natural abilities and roles, it is the woman's destiny to fight alongside the men of her generation. This purpose hidden within her design will protect him from his enemies and help him accomplish his mandate of headship.

God created Eve to be a capable, intelligent force to be reckoned with, as He did you. Although He created her to be weaker physically, God put within her something so powerful that even the devil is wary of it. This explains why the enemy would seek to corrupt her at the very moment she was taken out from Adam.

The irony is that Eve's introduction to the world achieved quite the opposite goal of helping Adam fulfill his God-given destiny. Instead, she went against Adam's instruction, took of the forbidden fruit, and offered it to him. Adam, not yet deceived, passively took the fruit without exerting his stand and protecting the woman and the territory God had for him. His action plunged the rest of mankind into a downward spiral of sin and shame. Humankind's innocence was compromised, and for the first time, Adam and Eve knew they were naked and were ashamed. Even today, some men still blame women for the conditions of the world because of Eve's actions.

For a long time and to this day, preachers have linked Eve's actions to her pride and her desire for independence. However, at Adam and Eve's point of temptation, sin had not yet entered the world and humankind still had its innocence. The serpent came and planted in Eve the idea that the fruit, once eaten, would make her be like God in that it would give her wisdom to know good and evil.

Genesis 3:6

So when the woman saw that the tree was good for food, that it was pleasant to the eyes, and a tree desirable to make one wise, she took of its fruit and ate. She also gave to her husband with her, and he ate.

The Bible does not say that Eve wanted to be independent of God (unlike Lucifer). The Bible says she wanted to be *like* God and to be wise!

When women refuse to submit and men refuse to lead and protect, the world plunges into total chaos!

Eve The Last

Desiring to be like God was not her crime. Does the Bible not tell us that we are to be Godlike? What about wanting to be wise—is that wrong? Clearly, we are asked to pursue wisdom. Proverbs 4 tells us that wisdom is the principal thing and that in all our getting, we must get understanding (wisdom). So, Eve was not wrong to desire to be like God or to be wise.

What Eve failed to do was submit to the delegate authority over her and follow his instruction to not eat of the tree of the knowledge of good and evil; she listened to the serpent instead. What about Adam's undoing? It was his refusal to lead, teach, and protect her! When women refuse to submit and men refuse to lead and protect, the world plunges into total chaos! As it was in the Garden of Eden, so it has been in every generation thereafter—women struggle to submit and follow, and men struggle to lead and protect.

Born out of wedlock without the love of a father, coupled with the effects of a mother who suffered from chronic rejection, conditioned me to not depend on others. Life's experiences persuaded me that people are generally not trustworthy and that they will leave you whenever things are hard. Nobody fights for you, only you can fight for yourself. Unbeknownst to me, I had come into agreement with the spirit of abandonment and rejection; this nearly shipwrecked my relationship with Derek when we dated.

I cannot remember what we argued about one day, but I was inconsolable. Derek, exasperated, decided it would be best if we went home to calm down and reconvene our discussion later. He had turned to walk back to his car when I heard clearly in my mind (for the first time!) abandonment saying, "See, they (the men) all walk away." That was my wake-up call; that day, I saw clearly what was hindering me from building a healthy relationship with Derek. *My sense of abandonment and rejection will never allow me to give myself fully to the man that I love, I thought. And definitely, it will be a major roadblock to trust him and be one with him if we are ever to tie the knot!*

That day, I had to deal with my real enemy and take back the ownership of my thoughts and heart. I had to surrender my life to Him before I could surrender my life to the one that I was going to marry.

It is time to bring back order and take on the role that God has designed us to play. We need to be this gift to our men—our brothers, husbands, leaders, or pastors. When we have issues against the men in our lives, we can never serve them with our gifts. If we do, it will most likely be because we need their approval or want to exert our control over them. When we fully surrender to God, we can then submit to the delegated authorities in our lives. We must understand that we are not created as an afterthought; the reverse is true. We have been fearfully and wonderfully made and intricately designed to be a wonderful gift and a capable warrior.

> **When we have issues against the men in our lives, we can never serve them with our gifts.**

What kind of warrior was Eve designed to be, and what is she capable of doing? I believe that Eve was primarily designed to war in the unseen world. Her weapon of warfare? Wisdom! Notice that the serpent did not come to Adam, but the enemy targeted Eve, knowing very well that she was intrigued by the fruit "that will make one wise." God intended for Eve to be the voice of wisdom in the lives of the people in her generation. She was to develop the ability to discern the presence of evil and help navigate the people out of danger and into the presence of good and ultimately of God.

Eve ^The Last

God's kind of wisdom is more than knowledge; it is beyond having the knowledge and understanding to recognize the right course of action and having the will and courage to follow it. It is knowing how to operate to get into God's order and aligning ourselves in accordance to His will, as revealed in the Bible. With order comes anointing. When anointing flows, we receive heavenly strategies and divine grace to operate our assignments, thus attracting success and favor into our lives. As believers, we are promised that blessings will follow us, but we must first come into agreement with God's way of doing things.

God's original intention was not for Adam and Eve to receive the knowledge of good and evil through experience but through divine revelation! It was not called the "tree of wisdom" but the "tree of the knowledge of good and evil." Eating of the fruit of the tree enabled Adam and Eve to know good and evil. However, wisdom is not knowing good and evil. Wisdom is knowing good *from* evil. God intended for Adam and Eve to attain such knowledge but not by eating of its fruit. God wanted Adam to learn to respect the limits imposed and develop the discipline of obedience to abstain. God's original intention was for humankind to recognize the fact that all that is opposed to the will of God is an evil work to be avoided. But when man violates God's order, what is good is now evil and vice versa.

Eve ate the fruit that was "good for food" as suggested by Satan, yet it was not good at all because God forbade it. Adam and Eve did come to a new awareness of "good and evil." Take notice of what happened in the process; after eating the forbidden fruit, that which was "good" came to be looked upon as evil. When God made Adam and then his wife, they were good in His sight. They did not know shame though they were created naked. Their nakedness was good in their state of innocence. Yet, once they ate the fruit of that tree, their nakedness made them feel ashamed and they tried to cover themselves up. Their nakedness was no longer good but now evil. And the fellowship they enjoyed with God was most certainly good, but once they disobeyed Him, they tried to hide from His presence rather than enjoy it. Why? Because this "good" (of enjoying God) was now "evil." They knew good and evil, but now the labels had been switched. This is the beginning of chaos—the mother of all destruction.

Through their voluntary resistance to yield to the temptation, Adam and Eve would gain true freedom: the liberty to choose what is good and not evil. If Adam had learned how to discern evil through divine revelation and develop that maturity to choose good, he would have attained Godlike knowledge of good and evil.

But as Adam failed to keep this divine appointed way and instead ate the forbidden fruit in opposition to the command of God, the power imparted by God to the fruit manifested in a different way. Adam learned the difference between good and evil from his own guilty experience. Understand that the tree has no demonic power and its fruit is not poisoned, but the very thing that was meant to help him attain true freedom has brought nothing but a sham liberty of sin, and with it death. This is all because man chose to obtain what God had portioned for him his way rather than God's way.

Although Eve failed and was tempted, we must understand that this did not change God's original intent for her. The Bible says, *"For the gifts and calling of God are irrevocable"* (Rom. 11:29).

Women and Wisdom

Heidi Lee, author of *Wisdom Is a Woman*, says, *"Wisdom is a woman. That is not just my opinion or some new academic theory. Wisdom is a woman because the Bible tells us so. It tells us that wisdom is more than just a benefit or a characteristic. In the Bible, wisdom is sometimes a person. When so personified, wisdom is always a woman. Sometimes she is Lady Wisdom. Sometimes she is Madame Insight. Most often she goes incognito; yet the shadow she casts is always a female form."*

Many women from the Bible are depicted as being wise. Defined by Proverbs and personified as female, wisdom is mature, sensible, and full of truth and knowledge; wisdom is strong, understanding, and follows justice. A common thread runs through the stories of all these women— their total allegiance to God and His ordained authorities!

Deborah

According to the book of Judges, Deborah was a prophetess of the God of the Israelites, the fourth judge of premonarchic Israel, and the only female judge mentioned in the Bible. She is the wife of Lapidoth. Deborah is one of the most influential women of the Bible. She is known for her wisdom and courage and for being the only woman of the Old Testament who is recognized for her own faith and action, not for her relationship to her husband or another man. Through her wisdom and prophetic utterance, she invoked courage in Barak to lead a victorious attack against the forces of Jabin, king of Canaan, and his military commander, Sisera. Despite Deborah's power and influence, she submitted herself under Barak and did not attempt to take credit for the victory. What about her husband, Lapidoth? The Bible did not say much about this man, but if you know anything about the culture of that day, you will understand that Lapidoth was no ordinary man. In fact, for Deborah to do what she did, he would have to be a countercultural man way ahead of his time.

In ancient Israel, Jewish culture was one of the most male dominant in the world. In ancient Judaism, a woman had rights only in the home and even that was very limited! The man had authority over his wife and daughters, dictating their activities and their relationships. A woman was passed from the control of her father to the control of her husband, with little or no say in the matter. They were sold for a dowry settlement, usually at the time of their coming of age. Women were not allowed to hold a significant role in the synagogue because they were "levitical-ly unclean" for several days every month during their menstrual cycle. Women were not regarded as members in a synagogue count. They were allowed to receive very little education on only religion, and men gave the main religious instruction in the home. They could not be disciples of any great rabbi; they certainly could not travel with any rabbi. So, you see, for Deborah to know and understand the law and ordinances of God to rule a nation, I believe that had to be Lapidoth's work.

Lapidoth was a picture of the Lord Jesus, who was radical in His teaching. He was not one to show partiality. In fact, many women followed Jesus … including prostitutes. He taught them, healed them, and released them into ministry. Many women were His disciples and supported Him not only in deeds but with their money as well. For the nation of Israel to listen and submit to Deborah's authority, apart from her wisdom and gift, I presume she must have been a submitted wife and endorsed by her husband. Her knowledge of the law of the land must have very likely come from her husband, who taught her. This serves as a beautiful picture of God's original intent for how men and women should relate, a picture that is not reserved for a marriage only.

E the Last ve

Rahab

The book of Joshua introduces us to one of the most thought-provoking, astonishing heroines of the Old Testament. That woman is Rahab, the prostitute of the Canaanite city of Jericho, who ultimately is noteworthy for her great faith and place in the lineage of Jesus Christ. But a closer examination of the life of this remarkable Gentile woman leads to deeper insights into the power of wisdom found in a woman. Rahab ran an inn, built on the Jericho city wall, where she hid the Israelite spies in her rooftop. When the king of Jericho learned that the men had been to Rahab's house, he ordered her to turn them over. She lied to the king's soldiers concerning the whereabouts of the spies and sent them off in the opposite direction. She made a pact with the two spies that they would spare her and her household when they attacked Jericho.

Spiritually, Rahab was not in an ideal circumstance to come into faith in the one, true God, the God of Israel. She was a citizen of a wicked city that God had condemned. Rahab was part of a corrupt, depraved, pagan culture. She had not benefited from the godly leadership of Moses or Joshua. However, she had one asset: wisdom! From many men, she had heard that the Israelites were to be feared. She heard the stories of their escape from Egypt, the crossing of the Red Sea, the wanderings in the wilderness, and their recent victory over the Amorites. She learned enough to reach the correct, saving conclusion: *"For the Lord your God is God in heaven above and on the earth below"* (Josh. 2:11). This change of heart, this faith—coupled with the actions prompted by faith—saved her and her family. Her wisdom prompted her to choose the winning side that made her and her family the only ones who survived the bloodshed amongst her countrymen. But the highlight must be that she eventually got grafted into the lineage of

Christ when she married Salmon, one of the two spies whom she had saved. Matthew 1 says, *"Salmon was the father of Boaz by Rahab, Boaz the father of Obed by Ruth, and Obed the father of Jesse."* Jesse was the father of King David, and out of the lineage of King David came our Savior and Lord, Jesus Christ.

We see the power of wisdom to rule and to save.

Let's look at the following story of an unnamed woman in the Bible. Her wisdom prevented a war and saved her whole city.

The Unnamed Maid Servant behind the Wall

Joab, the son of Zeruiah, was the nephew of King David and the commander of his army. King David appointed him to hunt down Sheba, who had raised a revolt against the king. Feeling the urgency to stop the revolt, Joab pursued Sheba to the city of Abel-beth-maachah, where they knew Sheba was hiding. They besieged the city. However, thanks to an unnamed, wise woman (whom the Bible addressed as a "maidservant"), Joab decided not to destroy Abel-beth-maachah because the city's people did not want Sheba hiding there. The whole negotiation happened behind the city wall, and Joab never even met this unnamed woman. She told the city's people to kill Sheba, and they threw his head over the wall to Joab. With that, Joab retreated with his assignment accomplished, King David's reputation preserved, and the city's residents relieved from the pain of warfare.

2 Samuel 20:22

*The woman, **with her wisdom**, came to all of the people in the city, and they cut off the head of Sheba the son of Bikri. When they threw it to Joab,*

he blew the horn, and they dispersed from the city, each going to his own tent.
Joab returned to Jerusalem to the king.

Wisdom is not reserved for only women but for men as well. But for women, the book of Genesis provides us with a hint of woman's innate desire for wisdom and how it may very well be the key to unlocking her destiny. Having said that, we must all agree that the biblical kind of wisdom starts with God and we only receive it through our reverence of Him.

Their source of wisdom and discernment must come from God and not just experience and their opinion.

Proverbs 1:7

Wisdom begins with the fear of the Lord, but fools despise wisdom and instruction.

Women who want to be an effective warrior for God must set their foundations right. Their source of wisdom and discernment must come from God and not just experience and their opinion. Luke 11:35, in The Passion Translation, instructs us to open our hearts, consider God's Word, and not mistake our opinions for revelation-light! The true wisdom of God will not violate His Word and His divine order. When the Word of God becomes our guidepost, we can birth forth revelation wisdom. When we fully embrace the Word of God as absolute truth and our hearts are locked in to what it says about who we are and how He loves us, we are now ready to be the wise warrior for Him. Know that unless your heart is protected by the Word and strengthened by God's love, you cannot perform your greatest assignment, which is to protect his heart.

Protect His Heart

Proverbs 31:10-11 (TPT)

Who could ever find a wife like this one?
She is a woman of strength and mighty valor!
She's full of wealth and wisdom.
The price paid for her was greater than many jewels.
Her husband has entrusted his heart to her,
for she brings him the rich spoils of victory.

Proverbs 31 talks about this *woman of valor* who is adorned with wealth and wisdom, but the greatest compliment must be that the man in her life can trust her with his heart. I found an interesting read from the site *The Good Men Project* about the man's heart: *"Have you seen a man's heart? So slow and sluggish, but oh so strong. With shackles and bindings, still it yet beats. Somehow, he maintains his purpose and passion. He is capable of such great things, marvels beyond compare, wonders that never cease … If you see a man whose heart is free, flee as far and as fast as you can because an encounter with this man will leave you forever changed. A man whose heart is truly free is the most dangerous thing in existence; he is a dreamer, a visionary, an idealist. This is a man who still sees all that is good in the world; he will shine a light on all that you find dim and dark and show you the beauty that lies underneath. This is a man who believes he can make the world a better place; he will touch you with his love for this world and you will believe also that the world can be changed. This is a man who burns with a passion so deep it cannot be extinguished; a man who creates miracles and makes his very dreams come true."*

What a beautiful description of the man's heart. Clearly, the hearts of men and women are structured differently; both are made strong and filled with great visions and passions. However, each handles distress and disappointments in different ways. While the woman's heart is soft and flexible, the man's heart is strong yet when broken shatters into pieces.

Eve The Last

What, then, are some of the key differences between males and females? In his book *Secure Daughters, Confident Sons* (Chapter One, "What Makes a Good Man?" and Chapter Two, "What Makes a Good Woman?"), author Glenn Stanton lists some distinctive traits characteristic of men and women, respectively. These lists are not intended to be exhaustive; obviously, each individual is unique. Based on what Stanton wrote for Focus on the Family, he listed a male's orientation toward life, which apparently tends to be outward. This is what they found out:

- **Explorative.** Every boy and every man are on a quest. Each discovers his identity "out there" in the world where he senses his larger purpose and destiny lie.

- **Determined to "deliver the goods."** A man places great stock in knowing that he has what it takes to complete the quest and accomplish the task at hand.

- **Needs to know what's next.** Unlike a woman, he isn't inclined to "cuddle," to "savor" meaningful experiences, or to "linger" in the moment. Generally speaking, he's anxious to move on to the next thing.

- **Opportunistic.** To put it another way, the male is a doer; and in the final analysis, his feelings about what he's doing or his reasons for doing it are less important to him than the urge and the opportunity to get it done.

- **Takes chances.** To seize and make the most of his opportunities, a boy or a man must be willing to take chances. Accordingly, a propensity to run a certain degree of risk is fundamental to the male character.

- **Initiator.** All of this presumes a certain willingness and ability to "take the bull by the horns" and make things happen. It also suggests that leadership, while not necessarily an exclusively male prerogative, is nevertheless more deeply rooted in the nature of men and boys.

- **Active and aggressive.** There's an obvious connection between initiation and active aggression. In light of this, it's interesting to note that the male brain is two-and-a-half times larger and more vital in the center and more devoted to aggression and action than the female brain.

- **Competitive and dominant.** Men want the best and will expend incredible energy toward getting it.

Men are wired to lead, conquer, and take territory just like what God intended in Genesis. While Eve was still in Adam, God spoke to man and mandated him to be fruitful and multiply, to fill the earth and subdue it and have dominion over all creation. Though God ordained men and women to lead, they were designed to lead differently and in different dimensions. Generally, men are built strong in physique and emotions to forge forward and take ground. They are driven by what they see and strive to overcome obstacles so that they can inherit the "land" of their promise. Hence, it is imperative that men be bold and courageous and their hearts be strong. They have been designed to lead, especially to lead the women and the children at home and in our communities in general. They gain courage to lead through the love and respect of those who they are called to lead. Through the victory in their quest, they gain much fulfillment, yet it is through the respect from the women they lead that they find courage to overcome the worst of situations and enemies! When that respect is withheld, it breaks men's hearts and takes away their ability to have courage. When their hearts break, they lose the ability to "see" and do not know how to fight.

Eve The Last

Acts 2:17

And it shall come to pass in the last days, says God,
That I will pour out of My Spirit on all flesh;
Your sons and your daughters shall prophesy,
Your young men shall see visions,
Your old men shall dream dreams.

In Acts 2, the Lord prophesied what would happen to the people of God when the Holy Spirit comes upon them after His death. Though men and women shall prophesy, the Lord emphasized that men would have their visions and dreams restored. So, when sin entered mankind, men's ability to see what God sees and dream the dreams of God disappeared. Men, created with power and strength, are robbed of their destiny to have dominion if they cannot see. A man sees with his heart, but God has given the secret power of his heart to the charge of the woman he is to lead. She is to protect his heart. Let's look at the story of Samson and Delilah ...

Samson and Delilah (Judges 16)

Samson's birth was announced by an angel during a dark time for the Israelites. Israel was under the rule and oppression of the Philistines. Samson was born a Nazirite and was set apart with supernatural physical strength from God to deliver and rule the nation of Israel. His supernatural strength lay in his hair, which had to remain uncut as a sign of consecration to the Lord. Strong as he was physically, Samson had a weakness for beautiful women. Though consecrated at birth, he did what pleased him when it came to the matter of his heart. He even pursued foreign women against the will of God. Judges 14 tells us of how he saw a woman of Timnah and fell head over heels in love with her and demanded to have her for a wife. During his wedding feast, he gave the guests a challenge with a promise of a reward. His wife, pressured by her countrymen, pestered him for seven days and manipulated him with her tears for the answer to his riddle. Samson gave in and lost the bet. He stormed back to his father's house only to find when he returned that his father-in-law had given his wife away to his best man. Samson was so humiliated that he killed 1,000 Philistine men with the jawbone of a donkey.

His trouble with women did not end there. Subsequently, Samson fell in love with a beautiful Philistine woman named Delilah. Philistine rulers came to Delilah and offered her money if she could find out what made Samson so strong. Twice Delilah tried to seduce and manipulate Samson into revealing the secret of his supernatural power. However, she could not deceive him. He tricked her with false information and when the enemies came to ambush him, he freed himself and escaped. Despite not being deceived and knowing that Delilah did not have his best interest at heart, Samson did not leave her. Finally, on her last attempt, the Bible says that Delilah's constant nagging so vexed Samson that he lost his grip on his heart and eventually told her the truth about his hair. That evening as Samson slept, Delilah cut his hair and called in the Philistines. The Philistine men captured Samson. Judges 16:21 says, *"Then the Philistines took him and put out his eyes, and brought him down to Gaza."*

While Adam fought for the things that are seen, Eve was wired to fight for the things that are unseen.

Have you ever wondered why they would gouge his eyes out, as that had nothing to do with his ability? I believe God wants us to understand the symbolism here. When a man's heart gives way, his vision in life is the first to fade away. So, as the wise warriors appointed by God in our generation, we need to protect the hearts of the men in our lives so that they can align themselves with God's vision and dreams for them. Along with the men, we can take the grounds that Satan has stolen from us and defeat the works of darkness that have come to bring chaos and sorrow.

Eve was created to be the warrior for Adam. While Adam fought for the things that are seen, Eve was wired to fight for the things that are unseen. While Adam was built with power and a natural inclination to dominate the world he was entrusted, he was, however, vulnerable to Eve, who was created to be his helper. Man and woman working in agreement together will form a formidable team to establish the dominion that God wants to see on this earth.

When God called me to Bible school, He only told me to be prepared. Little did I know what I was preparing for. Looking back, I doubt I would have been able to journey with Derek and everything that he was called to do if I had not given that year, 1998, to the Lord. It was not so much the doctrine and biblical history that God needed for me to learn but rather the person I had to become. In that year, God began to expose what was in my foundation. Though I love God, I had to learn to abandon my security from this world and trust Him totally. I remember coming out from school one day and I had only eighty cents in my pocket for lunch. With tears in my eyes, I had felt like what the apostle Paul said, *"I know both how to be abased and I know how to abound. Everywhere and in all things I have learned both to be full and to be hungry, both to abound and to suffer need"* (Phil. 4:12). This was the year that I learned to abandon myself and put on Christ and make that my motto in life.

God was the matchmaker who brought Derek and me together, but both of us have to continuously choose God and each other. Hence, when God put us together in marriage and in ministry, we decided to fight for each other. Derek fights for my honor, and I fight to protect his heart. When we stand with each other, with God at the center, we have all the power to stand against Satan and his forces. We had the strength to come against popular opinions and build a Spirit-filled Word-based church that God had instructed. When we stand with each other and advocate God's holy ordinance in our home, we provide a hedge to shield our children from the craziness of their world.

Today's world is treacherous. Godly men must arise to protect the women and children. Godly women must arise to stand guard in the Spirit, speak courage into men's hearts, and guide and govern our young people.

Are you willing to fight alongside the Lord Jesus, whom you love, to bring back His order and power to this world? Will you put aside your agenda and fulfill His agenda to manifest the kingdom of God in your generation? I encourage you to be the warrior you are meant to be. Let's fight for what matters and what will impact our future generations and eternity!

Chapter 4

She Is an Extension of the Work of the Holy Spirit

John 14:26

But the Helper, the Holy Spirit, whom the Father will send in My name, He will teach you all things, and bring to your remembrance all things that I said to you.

In Genesis 2, the Hebrew word *ezer* means "helper" and is used to describe Eve. The Holy Spirit is another person in the Bible whom God names helper. However, in John 14:26, "helper" is the Greek word *"paraklētos,"* which translates as the following: called to one's aid; advocate, intercessor; a consoler or a comforter. In other words, the Holy Spirit is the paraklētos. Although different words are used to describe Eve and the Holy Spirit, many interesting similarities exist. I believe when you carefully consider such similarities, you will understand what you are truly called to do. God intentionally wired into the creation of women certain giftings and inclinations that allow her to be an extension of the work of the Holy Spirit on the Earth.

Understanding this helped me navigate through my journey as a wife and a mother. I learned that my power is needed primarily in the things unseen and my main jurisdiction is behind the curtain (again, it is not wrong for any woman to be in the forefront if her work or ministry requires that of her). I stopped trying to stand out to avoid feeling invisible or lesser in importance. On the other hand, I started becoming more attuned to the things of the Spirit while fulfilling my earthly role as a wife and a mother. Not only did this bring about a greater level of liberty to be who I am, Derek and I found a greater synergy working together as well, and most importantly, I began to have a deepened intimacy with the Holy Spirit. Through that, God began to progressively download to me the mystery of the design of woman and her assignment in the end-time.

Someone wrote, *"Woman was not made to till the soil, she was not made to build the house, she was not made to steer the crane, nor stack the brick, nor hew the stones, nor build the road, nor head the state, nor lead the church, nor reap the harvest. It is woman's job to determine the atmosphere while the soil is being tilled. It is woman's job to determine the atmosphere while the house is being built. Though it is not her job to steer the crane, it is her job to make happy the one who steers the crane. It's not her job to stack the brick nor hew the stone; it's her job to make a wonderful spirit and atmosphere while the brick is being stacked and the stone is being hewn. It's not her job to build the road, nor head the state, nor lead the church, nor reap the harvest. Everywhere woman has ever been, it has been her job to provide the spirit of atmosphere while man does his work and changes the course of history."*

With societal advancements, availability of education, and equal opportunities, many women can lead companies, drive cranes, and build homes, and a handful may find their way to the top to lead churches or even head the state! Many women in the past did great things to change the course of history. And no matter what role women play, we always set the atmosphere where we operate; an office atmosphere is determined more by the spirit of the secretaries than that of the bosses and a mother and wife more determines the atmosphere of a home than a father and husband or the children. Your husband comes home at night, and the first thing he wonders is, *What mood is she in?* Your mood brightens or saddens his evening! Why? Because a man does not determine the mood of the house, you do!

The Bible commands us to exalt the Lord; it is the Holy Spirit who gives us the ability to exalt Him. Our Heavenly Father is the Great, Omnipotent God, but it is the Holy Spirit who causes us to be aware of God's power. The gospel brings salvation, but the unseen power of the Holy Spirit convicts the hearts of the hearers and activates their faith to receive. The presence of the Holy Spirit opens the door of heaven and causes heaven to penetrate the hearts of men so they can know God's presence, love, and power. The Holy Spirit leads the church to engage the community and bring about revival; this power is from the unseen One, the Holy Spirit!

The Holy Spirit has no form and we cannot see Him, yet His power is undeniable in our lives. He does not speak on His own but only what He hears from the Father and the Son. His role is not to exalt Himself but to be that help for God who brings God's people into spiritual maturity and power! God created Eve to help Adam. Both were to glorify God but in different roles and functions. Eve's role is very much like that of the Holy Spirit—working behind the scenes to bring about the manifestation of God's peace, presence, and power. If you do not understand your role as the extension of the work and power of the Holy Spirit, you will often feel overlooked and underappreciated. We were not put on Earth to exalt ourselves, earn others' praises, or make our names famous (though there is nothing wrong with that if God is the one who promotes you). Your gifts and talents will open doors for you, and God will promote you to fulfill His purpose. However, making our names great is not our end goal. Our end goal, like the Holy Spirit's, is to make great the name of our Lord and Savior, Jesus Christ!

So, ladies, you are the essence of the Holy Spirit in your home. Your church atmosphere often showcases the kind of women who worship there. God has put within you such sensitivity that you connect easily to the things of the spirit realm. You are naturally wired to be prophetic and, with a pure heart, have a heightened awareness of God's presence. If you want to know your duties in life, you must understand the function of the Holy Spirit. The Bible says that the Holy Spirit comforts, teaches, instructs, and leads; we are capable of doing the same. God used similar words to describe the purpose of Eve and the Holy Spirit. This same description applies to what is said about who God created you to be. You are a representative of the Holy Spirit in your home and in the body of Christ. By the power of the Holy Spirit, you too can comfort, lead, teach, and help in your family, church, and community.

The Role of the Holy Spirit and Women

I am not suggesting that we are called to perform every role of the Holy Spirit. However, some roles are similar and in line with the abilities that God has generally wired into women. These roles pertain to both men and women, but I am highlighting some that are generally more predominant for the women than the men.

She Loves with Her Whole Heart

Romans 5:5

Now hope does not disappoint, because the love of God has been poured out in our hearts by the Holy Spirit who was given to us.

One of the Holy Spirit's main roles is to give God's people a revelation of the love of the Father and the Lord. Although men and women are called to love, we express our love differently. A man's love is strong and involves less of his emotions. Women, however, are created with a full range of emotions and tend to be more sensitive to God's love and more open to express the love they feel. Men and women must learn to display the tender love God has for His people. One of Jesus's assignments was to present the Father's love to the world. In John 17:23, Jesus says, *"And that the world may know that You have sent Me, and have loved them as You have loved Me."* Hence, as women, we should openly express God's love not only to our husbands and children (as cited in Titus 2) but also to the people that God would send our way. Through our display of love we act as an extension of the Holy Spirit to bring about this revelation of the Father to a world hungry for His love.

According to Luke 7:38, a Pharisee invited the Lord Jesus to his home for a meal. Jesus obliged, and while he was there, an unnamed woman, known only as a "sinner" in her city, approached him with an alabaster flask of fragrant oil. She did what no person of that time would think of doing; she kneeled before Jesus, weeping and washing his feet with her tear-soaked hair, then she kissed his feet and broke the alabaster flask, pouring out the fragrant oil. What an open display of affection! How brave she was to do that! This "sinner" not only gave away the most expensive possession of her life, symbolically, she gave up the most important thing for a woman in that day.

During those biblical times, when a young woman arrived at the age to marry, the family would purchase an alabaster box for her and fill it with ointment; the size of the box and value of the ointment symbolized the amount of wealth her family had acquired. When a man would ask for her to marry him, she would break this precious box at his feet; moreover, the expensive ointment on his feet was meant to show him honor. So, when she decided to break her alabaster box for the Lord, it was a sign of honor. By doing so, she publicly displayed her devotion to the Messiah and pledged her total allegiance to Him. The revelation of how much she had been loved by Jesus unleashed boldness and courage to break away from the social norm of that time. In those days, it was socially unacceptable for any woman, and certainly not a woman regarded as a sinner, to show up in a men's meeting or to touch a man, and especially a rabbi who was a holy man. Imagine those darting eyes that followed her every move when she entered the room full of powerful "holy" men; yet she was brave enough because her heart was bursting with love for the One who is truly holy. She had her eyes set on the Lord in the room, and at that moment the world faded into the background.

> God created Eve to be drawn and fueled by love, first for God and then for her husband.

A woman's assignment, like the Holy Spirit's, is to fill her home with the fragrance of the love of God. God created Eve to be drawn and fueled by love, first for God and then for her husband.

Lao Tzu says, "Being deeply loved by someone gives you strength, while loving someone deeply gives you courage." I believe it is hard to love someone deeply and fearlessly without first experiencing being deeply loved by someone else; that kind of love can only originate from the greatest lover of the universe, which is God Himself. The love we have for another human is constantly tested by personal conflicts, misunderstandings, and just plain character weaknesses. When that love fails, God's love will continue to undergird us in these relationships, helping us to continue to love and honor each other despite trying circumstances.

Thankfully, I married a man who has an intimate walk with God and is not restrained in expressing God's love through him. We do not have major issues in our marriage, and we try our best to always come into agreement on matters whether big or small. Of course, in our twenty years of marriage, crises have happened, but we have chosen to love each other in spite of the situation. I remember a couple of years ago when Derek took an unnecessary investment risk and lost most of our savings for our children's education. That plunged him into total despair, and I felt the deep pain of losing so much money—a six-figure savings! Yet, that day when he sat on the bed in tears over this, I did not utter a word of condemnation. I put my arms around him and comforted him. That day, I chose the love and compassion of my Father rather than my own pain and disappointment. That day, I chose to stand with Derek and take the blow with him rather than be the source of an additional blow on him. He had decided to invest, and I did not stop him. To me, I had provided implied consent and I am responsible as well. That day, I chose him over money. I chose love over anger. I chose God over me.

She Comforts and Counsels with the Word of God

John 14:26 (AMP)

But when the Father sends the Comforter instead of Me—and by the Comforter I mean the Holy Spirit—he will teach you much, as well as remind you of everything I myself have told you.

While the New King James Version refers to the Holy Spirit as the *Helper*, the Amplified version refers to him as the *Comforter*. Another role of the Holy Spirit is to bring comfort to the world by reminding people what the Lord has said. God knows there will be times of troubles and people need to anchor their faith. The Bible says faith comes by hearing and hearing by the spoken Word (*Rhema*) of God. The New Testament disciples were constantly "hearing" through the Holy Spirit what the Lord said to them while He was still on Earth; the same is true today. The Holy Spirit speaks to God's people through impressions, inspirations, and inner convictions to bring to their remembrance all that Jesus spoke.

In various other Bible translations, the word *Counselor* appears instead of *Comforter*. The world's definition of comforting is this: to bring about consolation. However, biblical comforting involves more than soulish consolation. The Holy Spirit comforts people by bringing them back into faith, hope, and love by reminding them of God's promises. John 1 declares, *"In the beginning was the Word, and the Word was with God, and the Word was God. He was in the beginning with God. All things were made through Him, and without Him nothing was made that was made. In Him was life, and the life was the light of men."* Therefore, our foundation must be Jesus, who is the Word of God. When we counsel and bring to life the promises of God, the person who is grieving will then receive the "light" of the Word and be comforted. Herein lies the problem. When the Word of God and our obedience to the Word is no longer the foundation of our Christian faith, the Word then becomes power-less to comfort anyone. Special circumstances may require seeking professional counsel and more so medical assistance; however, when we adhere to the Word of God and follow the leading of the Holy Spirit, we will receive health both in the soul and body.

> **The degree by which you walk out the instructions of God is the same degree of power you will have to comfort and counsel the people of God.**

Proverbs 4:20-22

My son, give attention to my words;
Incline your ear to my sayings.
Do not let them depart from your eyes;
Keep them in the midst of your heart;
For they are life to those who find them,
And health to all their flesh.

A woman of God who desires to fulfill her destiny and be the extension of the work of the Holy Spirit must be founded in the Word. The degree by which you walk out the instructions of God is the same degree of power you will have to comfort and counsel the people of God. Notice what John 16 and Ephesians 1 says about the Spirit of God.

John 16:12-14

I still have many things to say to you, but you cannot bear them now. However, when He, the Spirit of truth, has come, He will guide you into all truth; for He will not speak on His own authority, but whatever He hears He will speak; and He will tell you things to come. He will glorify Me, for He will take of what is Mine and declare it to you.

Ephesians 1:16-18

[I] do not cease to give thanks for you, making mention of you in my prayers: that the God of our Lord Jesus Christ, the Father of glory, may give to you the spirit of wisdom and revelation in the knowledge of Him, the eyes of your understanding being enlightened; that you may know what is the hope of His calling, what are the riches of the glory of His inheritance in the saints.

In like manner, to be effective in our role as comforter and counselor, we must learn to hear from the Holy Spirit and counsel others based on the Word of God and not according to our personal experiences. Our experiences can serve as a confirmation and encouragement, but God's Word must be the handlebar for the people to hold on to. Furthermore, we must avoid confusing our opinion with revelation. We must pray for the Holy Spirit to give us revelation and show us truth from God's Word.

God created Eve to bring Adam comfort so that he would not be alone. Unfortunately, she did not heed Adam's counsel, which came from God, and took the counsel of the deceiver, Satan. Whenever we violate God's instructions, we will expose ourselves to the lies of demons and jeopardize our assignment. Let us learn from Eve's mistake and not give heed to any voice or instruction that is not from God.

Amy (not her real name) was an enabler. She was raised in a family where she solved everyone's problems. She got so used to family members asking her for advice that she based her worth on her ability to be of help to everyone else. Everything was good until she got married. Mark (not his real name either) resented his wife's inability to say no to her extended family. He felt like the outsider in this marriage and over time developed a deep resentment toward Amy and her family. Ill-equipped to handle his emotions and deal with the chaos, he began to shut himself off and was constantly cutting in his responses. Amy was clueless about her husband's suffering and felt disrespected, which further enhanced her sense of unworthiness.

When I first met this couple and saw the personal dynamics between them, I knew something needed to happen in order for their marriage to heal. Without the healing, there would be no chance for oneness in this union. Instead of dealing with their behaviors, I expounded on God's idea of marriage through the Bible and revealed the sacredness of the marriage covenant. Through the Word, they began to realize the need to deal with the root issue and work toward building a marriage that pleased God and testified of Him.

Today, Amy and Mark have arrived at a place where they can openly express their love and respect for each other. Their marriage has brought so much healing to other marriages around them, and they are even trained to be marriage counselors!

She Intercedes with Her Voice

I overheard two women chatting in the market. One asked the other, "Does your husband talk to you?" Her companion answered, "Of course he talks. He has to ask me what's for dinner, doesn't he?"

Dr. Barton Goldsmith, an award-winning therapist and psychology writer, says, *"There are some other interesting facts that can enlighten us as to why it seems that 'men don't talk.' For example, women have twice as many words as men. Women speak at 250 words per minute and men speak at 125, and according to Gary Smalley, author of* Making Love Last Forever, *in the course of a day women speak 25,000 words compared to a man who only uses 12,000. It seems that by the end of the day men are talked out and women still have a day's worth of conversation in them. So, one of the reasons men don't feel comfortable talking is because most women can out talk them."*

He further expounds on the observation regarding the difference between a man and a woman as it pertains to thinking and feeling. *"It is interesting to note that women think and feel at the same time, while men can only think or feel. And based on most men's reluctance to embrace their feminine side, it's no wonder they do their best to stay in their heads."*[1]

Well, it's no wonder that man is unwilling to embrace his feminine side because most of it was removed with the creation of Eve! It is generally accepted that women are hardwired to be more talkative from the womb. Before we're even out in this world, our brains are programmed to be more talkative. When it comes to the makeup of our

---

[1] https://www.psychologytoday.com/us/experts/barton-goldsmith-phd

brains, women have something that can be referred to as an eight-lane interstate system that processes emotion, whereas men have something closer to a backcountry road. This means women are naturally more emotional, and that makes them much more talkative. In recent years, a gene called FOXP2 has come to be regarded by many scientists as essential for human speech. New research has shown that the building blocks of the gene are more abundant in young girls than boys, making the former more developed in their speech and language abilities. No matter what, we all can agree that women love to talk! It is in our design to communicate! In fact, that is how we share our life with people and especially with our significant others and bring them into our inner emotions. This is a major reason why we talk so much. This is also why when the men in our lives refuse (or when we deem they're refusing) to talk to us, we feel rejected and abandoned.

God gave women the ability to speak and communicate primarily not to rule over and correct the men but to express love, to comfort, and to counsel. However, I believe the most important spiritual assignment is to intercede for them in prayer. Look at what Romans says about the Holy Spirit in this respect.

Romans 8:25-27

But if we hope for what we do not see, we eagerly wait for it with persever-ance. Likewise the Spirit also helps in our weaknesses. For we do not know what we should pray for as we ought, but the Spirit Himself makes interces-sion for us with groanings which cannot be uttered. Now He who searches the hearts knows what the mind of the Spirit is, because He makes intercession for the saints according to the will of God.

From this passage, we see that the Holy Spirit has been given the assignment to intercede for the saints. As the extension of that assignment, women are called to travail in prayer and intercession for men and for whomever God has placed in their hearts.

Jeremiah 8:19

Listen! The voice,
The cry of the daughter of my people
From a far country:
"Is not the Lord in Zion?
Is not her King in her?"

There was a time recorded in the book of Jeremiah when God raised up a group of women to wail in intercession for the people to return back to the Lord. It was a time of great apostasy in the land of Judah where deception was rife. The only people who listened to God and the prophet Jeremiah were the wailing women. God gave these women a message, and He authorized them to proclaim this message in His name.

In Bible times, grieving was a communal activity. Professional wailing women were invited to funerals and other somber events to lead the community in shared expressions of grief. The wailing women played a therapeutic role in society. In Jeremiah 9, they also played a prophetic role. Tears give powerful, visible expression to the fact that everything is not as it should be. The wailing women challenge the complacency that ignores the many social injustices threatening the well-being of society as a whole. Being summoned by God to raise up a lament and to involve the

God created Eve with a greater capability to speak and express herself with words, making many of them effective in the area of prayer and intercession.

community by teaching their daughters and neighbors, the wailing women serve as God's spokespersons and as the people's conscience in protesting against the wrongs in their world. Receiving the Word from God's mouth, the wailing women call on the people to live in justice so that others may live as well.

God created Eve to be sensitive to the unseen world. While He wired Adam to conquer and advance the physical world, Eve was driven to run after the intangible things of God. God created Eve with a greater capability to speak and express herself with words, making many of them effective in the area of prayer and intercession.

When I first met Candice (not her real name), she had been a church leader for many years. However, she struggled in the area of finances and had a certain ideal regarding the lifestyle she desired. Hence, when her husband, who was unhappy with his then well-paying job, began contemplating a redirection in his vocation, her world was knocked off the edge. She began to nag her husband and even threaten him with the hope that he'd stay in his job for their financial security. Raymond (not his real name) felt trapped by guilt, resented the absence of his wife's support, and began to plunge into early depression.

When Candice sought counsel, I encouraged her to use her words not to stir up fear but to release faith. As she learned about the power of using her words to do good through releasing faith through intercession and edification, she began to see how she had transgressed against God. She had allowed materialism to control her life and the powers of darkness to divide her and her husband. She started to change her verbiage and channeled her attention on interceding rather than nagging. Fast-forward to today—Raymond is thriving in his new career and prospering more that he had imagined he could!

Interceding for His Vision

Acts 2:16-18

But this is what was spoken by the prophet Joel:
"And it shall come to pass in the last days, says God,
That I will pour out of My Spirit on all flesh;
Your sons and your daughters shall prophesy,
Your young men shall see visions,
Your old men dream dreams.
And on My menservants and on My maidservants
I will pour out My Spirit in those days;
And they shall prophesy."

We must uphold the men of every generation in prayer because God has given them the role of leading humanity and they need courage and strategy to fulfill the destiny God has for them. Praying for men to see God's vision and dream God's dream is probably the most crucial thing we can do. The key principle of successful leadership always begins with a vision. In Acts 2:16-18, we read about how the Holy Spirit empowers men to fulfill their headship; He bridges the mind of man with the mind of God. In doing so, He gives men the ability to prophesy of things to come, see visions, and dream dreams. He came to restore the vision of men so they can continue to fulfill their God-given mandate (Gen. 1:28) to be fruitful and fill the earth and subdue it, even in its fallen state.

When men cannot see what God is doing, their vision is reduced to mere sight. On this distinction between sight and vision, Max De Pree writes, *"We can teach ourselves to see things the way they are. Only with vision can we begin to see things the way they can be."*

In his book, *The 21 Indispensable Qualities of a Leader,* the final quality John C. Maxwell describes is ***vision***. While the other twenty qualities help us understand a leader's makeup, the final quality helps us understand what makes a leader attractive. Without vision, a leader cannot lead; vision is the quintessential piece of leadership. People don't stay on course for something they cannot see, and they don't give their best to something they cannot understand. You have to see the dream to seize it. A leader's responsibility is to see the vision and communicate it effectively so that the people he is leading can help him seize it. Nelson Mandela once said, *"Action without vision is only passing time. Vision without action is merely daydreaming. But vision with action can change the world."* God wants men to be bold and change the world. He created men with the ability to see what should be, and he created women to help them achieve those visions.

> A woman's role is to protect his heart; she fights to guard it, and with prayer she empowers the courage within him to bring to life what he envisions.

So, where does vision come from? Vision comes from within. John C. Maxwell says, *"You can't buy, beg, or borrow vision. It has to come from the inside."* Don't expect a vision to randomly fall from the sky. A leader will discover vision within his heart. A woman's role, as mentioned earlier, is to protect his heart; she fights to guard it, and with prayer she empowers the courage within him to bring to life what he envisions.

If you ask a man living an empty, dead-end life if he wishes he had a better life, he will certainly say yes. But while he may desire a better life, he has no vision for it. As he peers into his future, all he sees is more of his current circumstances. He's like the actor Bill Murray in the movie *Groundhog Day* living the same day over and over. Your vision is not merely your wants, wishes, and desires. Your vision is what you see, and what you see will determine the direction of your future. There's nothing more frustrating than a leader who cannot clearly articulate why they're doing what they're doing. Quite commonly in marriages, the wife takes over the leadership of her household. She takes on the responsibility not only of the mundane, daily needs but also the spiritual direction of the family; this happens all while the husband focuses only on being successful in his work and bringing in financial provision. The husband's lack of interest in the things of God or the desire to spiritually lead his family is devastating and hinders the establishment of God's kingdom here on Earth.

God is very interested in a person's capacity for vision. Repeatedly in the Bible, God asks people, *"What do you see?"* By saturating our minds with Scripture, our capacity for vision will be enhanced. Disciplined Scripture reading is essentially reading God's thoughts, and it expands our capacity to know and think the thoughts of God and therefore transcend conventional limitations. Although our eyes allow us to see what is, vision is the pathway by which we can see ... and help others see ... what can be. Human beings are mysterious creatures who are powerfully affected by vision. We are designed in such a way that we will move in the direction of what we see. Your vision is your future, and your vision is your imagination. You need an imagination inspired by the thought of God and His promises. You need the eye of an eagle who builds its nest atop the highest mountain or rock. *"From there it spies out the prey; its eyes observe from afar"* (Job 39:29). God has not called you to be a chicken who pecks around in the barnyard of the status quo and never sees more than just the dust of Old MacDonald's farm. God has called men and women to mount up on eagles' wings and soar above the storms (Isa. 40:30-31). Knowing humanity's tendency to move independently of each other, God prominently gave men the vision of what is to come and women the vision of the unseen so that, together, they can reign and bring God's kingdom here on Earth. Eve was made to be the wind under Adam's wing. They were made to be united as one, to soar like an eagle, and to have dominion in the realm of the physical and of the spiritual. Adam was supposed to see ahead, and Eve was supposed to be his hindsight. Working as one, they would be unstoppable, and the devil would not have any chance to dominate.

In like manner, the church, being the bride of Christ, must fully comprehend and embrace the vision of its headship, who is our Lord, Christ. Abiding as one with Christ, the church will be empowered to bring God's kingdom order into the world, and the world will witness the manifestation of God's glory and blessings. Apart from the headship, the church will be disconnected from Christ's vision and will not have the power to perform its tasks. However, if properly connected, the church can fulfill its purpose. Although Eve was not created to be strong physically and emotionally, God gave her a strength in her spirit that could very well overwhelm any man. We find an example of this same strength in the person of Delilah.

Delilah

We read in the previous chapter about how Delilah, being a woman of little strength and low social status, managed to weaken the strongest man who ever lived. Judges 16 provides insight on this matter.

Judges 16:16

And it came to pass, when she pestered him daily with her words and pressed him, so that his soul was vexed to death …

Samson, despite his mighty strength, found himself trapped in a situation that he could not escape. The woman that he deeply loved overpowered him with her persistently nagging spirit; this resulted in

Samson losing his resolve and giving away the secret of his powerful physical strength. A man may be stronger than you physically and emotionally because men are, by nature, more emotionally stable, but you hold an unseen power that can destroy a man and this power is your spirit!

A woman can make Eden a paradise if she so chooses, or she can curse everything in it as Eve did. A woman can make an ark a life-saving boat and the Nile River a nursery, or she can curse her husband as in Job's ash heap. It's her choice! She can ruin a nation as Jezebel did, or she can change a house into a church like Priscilla did. She can make a worship service great by giving her all or ruin one by withholding as Sapphira did. She can fill the house with Mary's ointment, or she can fill it with Michal's hatred. She can save a nation as Esther did or she, like Jezebel, can destroy one. Even though God ordained man to be the leader, God has given to woman the power to influence the man's ability for greatness. The man may be the leader, but you are the one who will influence him to be good, great, or greater.

Unfortunately for Samson, he met his tragic end because the woman in his life did not care for his heart. Through her manipulative spirit, she took his vision and destroyed his spiritual calling. In my years of ministering to women, I have witnessed many who, because of wounds in life, learned the ungodly, unloving way of achieving their goals. They use tactics such as manipulation, seduction, and flattery to control their men to accomplish what they want. The end result is always a tragedy; the men lose their sight, shut down their hearts, and for some lose their ability to fulfill their calling.

God created Eve to fight for Adam and his vision. She desired to be wise so that she could be that help for him; for this cause, she took the fruit and offered it to Adam because she believed that in doing so they would receive wisdom. I believe her intention was never to rebel against

Eve The Last

God but to give Adam a gift that would help him. Unfortunately, Eve did not realize that the gift that Adam needed was not found in that fruit but what God had built in her, which needed to be developed!

Chapter 5

She Is a Mother

Whether or not you are a mother, God has created you with an innate maternal instinct. The world tries to make sense of this innate desire and call it the "biological urge." The world believes that as the physical body matures, women develop the instinct to have children. But no substantial evidence supports the notion that this biological maturation creates this deep longing for a child. The same goes for men; no qualifying evidence links biology to the creation of parental desire. So, what's behind the "urge"?

The world then tries to put the blame on the pronatalist movement, when society needed to encourage people to have lots of children. They claim that we have been brainwashed to think that having children leads to our fulfillment and is part of our destiny. So, is the "urge" brought about psychologically? I think not. After the creation of the first man and woman, God blessed them and commanded them to be fruitful and multiply after themselves so that their descendants could fill the earth (Gen. 1:28). God set that procreation mandate from the beginning, not only physically but spiritually.

In Matthew 28, Jesus instructed His followers, in what we know today as the great commission, to go therefore and make disciples of all the nations, baptizing them in the name of the Father and of the Son and of the Holy Spirit. Be it naturally or spiritually, God has designed in creation of mankind (and womankind) the desire to reproduce. God gave men the power of the seed, and to women He gave the privilege to carry that seed to fruition and maturity. Men and women find a great sense of fulfillment when they birth and raise a child, groom a person to maturity in the faith, or see the rise of their protégé in business or any area of interest.

Genesis 1:27

So God created man in His own image; in the image of God He created him; male and female He created them.

Although written in patriarchal contexts, the Bible does not refer to God exclusively in masculine metaphors. Some feminine metaphors are used to describe God. God carries both the masculine and feminine attributes, which we know from studying Genesis 1:27. God created man (Adam, who is male) according to his own image and likeness, and from man He also created woman (Eve, who is female); both were of human substance, but each of a different aspect of God's nature.

"People described God in feminine terms, not because God is actually a woman, but because feminine or maternal traits say something true about God and about their experience with God."[1] In several places, the Bible refers to God as a mother bird protecting its young.

Psalm 17:8

Keep me as the apple of Your eye;
Hide me under the shadow of Your wings,

---

[1] Japinga, *Feminism and Christianity*, p. 66

The same reference was made in Psalm 57:1, Psalm 91:4, and Ruth 2:12. Jesus uses these images when he laments over Jerusalem in the book of Matthew.

Matthew 23:37

O Jerusalem, Jerusalem, the one who kills the prophets and stones those who are sent to her! How often I wanted to gather your children together, as a hen gathers her chicks under her wings, but you were not willing!

While these images paint God as One who protects and shelters His people, Deuteronomy 32 describes God as an eagle who stirs up its nest and pushes the eaglets out, catching them before they fall. Hosea 13:8 further declares God to be like a bear who would attack any devourer who would rob Him of His cubs. Both passages paint God as determined and fierce to protect His people and to ensure that they grow up and grow strong to fight for themselves. In other words, the maternal nature of God both protects His people from harm and nurtures His people into spiritual maturity.

Deuteronomy 32:10-11

He found him in a desert land
And in the wasteland, a howling wilderness;
He encircled him, He instructed him,
He kept him as the apple of His eye.
As an eagle stirs up its nest,
Hovers over its young,
Spreading out its wings, taking them up,
Carrying them on its wings.

Eve The Last

Hosea 13:8

I will meet them like a bear deprived of her cubs;
I will tear open their rib cage,
And there I will devour them like a lion.
The wild beast shall tear them.

The prophet Isaiah, in particular, was fond to liken God to a human mother.

Isaiah 42:14

I have held My peace a long time,
I have been still and restrained Myself.
Now I will cry like a woman in labor,
I will pant and gasp at once.

Isaiah 66:13

As one whom his mother comforts,
So I will comfort you;
And you shall be comforted in Jerusalem.

Isaiah 49:15

Can a woman forget her nursing child,
And not have compassion on the son of her womb?
Surely they may forget,
Yet I will not forget you.

God created Eve to carry the maternal attribute of God. He designed her to protect and nurture the young. In Genesis 3:20, God referred to Eve as a mother before she ever had her first child. You see, you do not come into motherhood just by giving birth to a child; you are a mother by virtue of the fact that God has put this maternal gift into the spiritual DNA of all women in creation. This is probably the most powerful thing God has put inside of us. When we fully connect with our inner ability to nurture and provide care, such care will heal brokenness, which is prevalent in this hour of darkness.

The Lord prophesied to His disciples about the signs of the end-times. In Matthew 24, He said that one sign will be lawlessness making the love of many grow cold. However, a woman awakened to the maternal design of her creation can draw from the reservoir of God's love inside her to heal cold hearts and ignite His love within His people.

> **While the strategy of darkness is to divide and conquer, God's way is to unite and overcome.**

A healed heart will dream big dreams and accomplish what was never thought possible. A healed heart can trust God and follow His instructions. A healed people will find unity in the midst of differences. This gift of motherhood is most threatening to the power of darkness, and Satan is set to usurp and corrupt it. While the strategy of darkness is to divide and conquer, God's way is to unite and overcome.

Woman and Her Power to Unite

Eve provided valuable, vital strength to Adam. One of her roles as a significant helper for Adam was to unite the family to stand with him. While God ordained man to develop his vision and strength to protect his family, He ordained woman to nurture and unite her children to follow the headship of the family. Her ability to unite the family, and likewise the body of Christ, is a great threat to the devil.

Incapable of disarming the power of the church, the devil took to divide the people in the family and in the body, causing a short circuit in the power to stand against the evil schemes of the present times. Look at what the Bible says about the effects of division:

Mark 3:24-25

If a kingdom is divided against itself, that kingdom cannot stand. And if a house is divided against itself, that house cannot stand.

Unity is the prerequisite for power. Where there is unity, there is power, but when disunity resides, there will be powerlessness. Jesus, in John 17, prayed a priestly prayer over his disciples, frequently emphasizing his desire to see unity amongst His people, with Him, and with the Father. Why? God knows that men have the propensity to operate independently of each other. God desires for His people to live interdependent lives and trust who He is in each of them. That is why Adam should not be alone, nor did He create him to be self-sufficient. When a family unites their hearts and moves together, they create power to protect themselves and impact others. Likewise, a church is only as strong as the united families in it. Divided families weaken that resolve to trust each other and move together.

God duly noted in Genesis 11:6, *"Indeed the people are one and they all have one language, and this is what they begin to do; now nothing that they propose to do will be withheld from them."* In this story, determined men, out of their arrogance, came together to build a tower that would reach heaven. God remarked that it is not impossible for them to reach heaven with that tower! The key to achieving a corporate assignment is not nobility but in the presence of unity! As you can see, unity, regardless of the goal, catches the attention of God. However, as the men's intention to reach heaven came from pride and rebellion, God disrupted their progress by giving them different languages so they could not communicate to accomplish their goal.

A similar story in the New Testament tells of how God brought unity to His people to advance His plan. This story happened fifty days after the resurrection of Jesus. The disciples were told to wait for the power of the Holy Spirit to descend upon them so that they could witness the coming kingdom of God. In the Upper Room, we saw a beautiful picture of men and women praying together "in one accord" and the Holy Spirit came with power. They all began to speak in tongues they had not learned, worshipping and proclaiming the testimony of Jesus. A further read reveals that experience brought about great conviction and the disciples went out of the Upper Room, turning the world upside down with the gospel and signs and wonders! Opposite the story of the Tower of Babel, in the Upper Room, the believers found a common tongue and this ability would be the key to bring unity back to the House of God.

Ezekiel 37:17

Then join them one to another for yourself into one stick, and they will become one in your hand.

Your ability to fulfill your role as a mother (natural or spiritual) first comes from God.

God told Ezekiel to join the sticks together and write what God is saying with it. What kind of story can we write for God if we can unite the people of God? What can we build to glorify God? What power, sign, and wonder can we demonstrate if we can all agree? Psalm 133:1 declares, *"Behold, how good and how pleasant it is for brethren to dwell together in unity!"* Indeed, how would our world change if we, the women of the family of God, could dwell in unity? What kind of impact could that produce? I believe it would bring the power back to the body of Christ! Women have the power to unite others—men, women, and children. Eve has the power to unite the family and God's people, and this power comes from God.

Am/Em (Mother)

Letter	Name and pronunciation	Ancient pictogram and its meaning	Translation of the pictogram	Numeric meaning
א	**Aleph** aw'-lef		God the Father, deity, strength, leader, first	1
מ/ם	**Mem** mame		water, liquid, massive, chaos, raging	$\frac{13}{40}$

A look at the original pictographic script shows that the word "mother" is made up of two characters: ***Aleph*** and ***Mem***. *Aleph* is a picture of an ox. As the ox is strong, the letter also means strong. *Mem* is a picture of water. Putting the two characters together forms the phrase "Strong Water." Hence …

Mother = Strong Waters

Strong Waters = One Who Unites + Binds

The Hebrews made glue by boiling animal skins in water. As the skin broke down, a sticky, thick liquid formed at the surface of the water. This thick liquid was removed and used as a binding agent—"strong water." This is the Hebrew word meaning "mother," the one who "binds" the family together. Finally, "Aleph" carries the numerical number 1, which denotes "God," "Leader," and "First." Your ability to fulfill your role as a mother (natural or spiritual) first comes from God. You can lead your flock with the strength of God if He is your source.

Woman and Her Power to Nurture

No matter what season you are in, you do not have to wait to exercise the gift and the power of motherhood. Some people's lives will change because you are willing to be the extension of God's motherhood. The power of motherhood is not restricted to just protecting and healing; it carries the ability to nurture the people of God. The aim of nurturing is always to bring someone into maturity—both natural and spiritual maturity. For the purpose of this book, I want to focus on the spiritual aspect. What is the yardstick for maturity according to the Bible? Romans 8 plainly gives us the answer. The maturity of sonship is measured by the degree that a person is led by the Spirit and not his flesh. Hence, being led by the Spirit is the prerequisite for any woman who desires to nurture others. And the goal of any discipleship is for those who are discipled to learn to hear the voice of the Spirit and be willing to be led by Him.

Romans 8:14-15

For as many as are led by the Spirit of God, these are sons of God. For you did not receive the spirit of bondage again to fear, but you received the Spirit of adoption by whom we cry out, "Abba, Father."

Godly women, who will activate their motherly nature, will be instrumental in resisting the advancement of the works of darkness and will bring society back into hope and love.

Eve The Last

God instituted the role of women. He sees the function of the wife and mother as one of the best defenses against the plague of depression and hopelessness that we face today because of the extent of lawlessness in our society. Godly women, who will activate their motherly nature, will be instrumental in resisting the advancement of the works of darkness and will bring society back into hope and love. Let us take a look at some more examples of godly women.

Jerusha and Jedidah (2 Kings 15; 2 Kings 22)

The presence of a godly woman in a child's life can eradicate the effects of an absentee father and the bad influences of a culture.

Jerusha is an example of a godly woman. Second Kings 15 records that Jotham was a righteous king of Judah, and his mother's name was Jerusha, the daughter of Zadok the chief priest. Her outstanding contribution to society was to raise a son to have a steady character of a strong and wise leader—one who could turn God's blessing toward a whole nation.

Another godly woman was Jedidah, the wife of wicked king Amon. Jedidah accomplished the same to raise up godly children, as recorded in 2 Kings 22. Her son was Josiah, whose personal righteousness prolonged the life of Judah. Even though he had one of the most evil fathers (King Amon), he himself was a very righteous leader.

Jerusha and Jedidah had one thing in common: They found fulfillment in serving their families and pointing their children in the right direction. They prized obedient, stable children and believed that expanding and improving a child's mind was a full-time job. They strove to instill the godly values and the right perspectives in their children. The presence of a godly woman in a child's life can eradicate the effects of an absentee father and the bad influences of a culture.

Proverbs 29:15

The rod and rebuke give wisdom, but a child left to himself brings shame to his mother.

Why would a wayward child bring shame to his mother? A mother is deemed to play a significant role in her child's formative years. When a mother does not do quite as much as she should, the child's character and ability to choose right from wrong are hindered. However, fathers play a role in leading their children as well. When the father sets the vision and leads his household and the mother nurtures the children to take the lead from their father and develop their character, we see the formation of a powerful family that will define their society. Unfortunately, in this time of sexual immorality and social degradation, we see many single mothers leading and nurturing their children on their own. Though this is not the ideal arrangement, when a woman is willing to partner with the Spirit of God, her nurturing ability will make up for what is missing in that child's life.

Proverbs 29:17

Correct your son, and he will give you rest; yes, he will give delight to your soul.

Jochebed

Jochebed, better known as Moses's mother, a Levite, had married a Levite and given birth to a son in a most inconvenient time. The king of Egypt had instructed the termination of all Hebrew baby boys in the fear of their growing population and influence in the land. Jochebed, apparently a protective and witty woman, decided that she would do everything she could to protect her baby and nurture him to adulthood. She hid him for three months, and when she could no longer do so, she made a basket out of bulrushes and put him among the reeds by the riverbank. Intentionally, she instructed her daughter, Miriam, to ensure that the Pharaoh's daughter would find baby Moses and take pity on the Hebrew child. Miriam ensured that Pharoah's daughter found him. When that happened, Miriam jumped upon the chance and offered to find a nanny for the baby boy to look after him for her. Of course, the nanny was Moses's own mother! The Pharaoh's daughter not only instructed Miriam to take him and find a nurse for him, she even offered to pay for his care! What a brilliant plan! So, Miriam brought the child back to their mother, and she took him and nursed him.

The Bible does not say much about the kind of impact Moses's mother had on her son during his early years before she gave him over to Pharaoh's daughter. However, we can deduce from Moses's character and his compassion for the people of Israel that he knew his roots and had a great connection with the spiritual legacy of Israel. Although we know little about Moses's mother, we find great significance in her revealed actions toward her son. Not only did she care, protect, and provide for him in unique and creative ways, she also was an instrument of God's purpose in the life of Moses and the nation of Israel. As she lived out her life amid a rather desperate situation, she acted out of her faith in God, not in fear, and trusted God's work and leading. In this way, she served as the deliverer (so to speak) of the national deliverer of Israel, Moses. And as it turned out, the child she delivered would later deliver her and her people out of bondage and lead them toward the Promised Land.

Although our motherly care and acts toward our children may not occupy an equally central place in the salvation history of God's people, we never know what acts of faith may significantly impact future generations. So, consider the example of Jochebed and diligently pursue the purposes God has for you in the lives of your children! In like manner, as women of God, we also must not neglect our responsibility to nurture the young in faith in the kingdom of God. Besides men, God expects women to make disciples as well. The great commission given in Matthew 28:18 to raise up disciples was given to all and not just men. Titus 2 sheds some light on what God expected the role of older women to be toward younger women in the church.

Titus 2:3-5

The older women likewise, that they be reverent in behavior, not slanderers, not given to much wine, teachers of good things—that they admonish the young women to love their husbands, to love their children, to be discreet, chaste, homemakers, good, obedient to their own husbands, that the word of God may not be blasphemed.

As society progresses and the rising success of women in the marketplace and ministry continues, we see women mentoring men. If we truly understand the definition of discipleship, then we know that its purpose is not to lord over others or to clone them to be like us. Paul emphatically stated in 1 Corinthians 11:1, *"Imitate me, just as I also imitate Christ."* Hence, the end goal of discipleship is to train others to think and behave like Christ. We best achieve this through a mutual trusting relationship built between two parties. For the context of women who disciple, consider the Bible story that beautifully depicts the power and the tremendous blessing, to both the disciple and the disciples, when it is done in love and with mutual respect: the story of Naomi and Ruth. Their stories are woven together so closely that they are nearly inseparable. In fact, we know more about the relationship between these two women than we know about them individually. Their relationship offers a beautiful model of godly relationships—a stunning look at a blending of lives and the power of healthy discipleship.

Naomi

A famine in Canaan forced Elimelech and Naomi, along with their sons, to migrate from Bethlehem to Moab. Their sons married Moabite women, Orpah and Ruth. Elimelech passed away, and about ten years later, both of Naomi's sons died as well. Naomi, Ruth, and Orpah all became widows.

Naomi heard that the Lord helped the people of her homeland and food had been provided back home. She decided to go back to Bethlehem in Judah and told Orpah and Ruth to stay in Moab and find new husbands. While Orpah returned to her mother's home, Ruth clung to Naomi and told her that she would stay with her and that Naomi's God and people would be her God and people. This is the famous saying of Ruth to Naomi that reflected Ruth's character:

Ruth 1:16-17

But Ruth said:
"Entreat me not to leave you,
Or to turn back from following after you;
For wherever you go, I will go;
And wherever you lodge, I will lodge;
Your people shall be my people,
And your God, my God.
Where you die, I will die,
And there will I be buried.
The Lord do so to me, and more also,
If anything but death parts you and me."

Ruth is widely praised for her loyalty toward Naomi, and still today, many preachers and teachers of the Word reference Ruth when speaking of loyalty. While this is true, we must also understand that no one will follow a person who is not of noble character. To leave one's own country and people and cling to a foreign woman, who did not seem to have anything else to offer, speaks of something more. Naomi was clearly a noble woman who had built a strong relationship with Ruth. Even though Naomi left her homeland, she did not forsake her faith. One could guess that Naomi likely followed her traditions of worship and spoke openly of her faith to her foreign daughter-in-law, teaching her about the God of Israel and His faithfulness. Through Naomi, Ruth learned about the God of Israel and chose to put her trust in Him. And it is apparent that Ruth trusted Naomi greatly and followed her advice in the way she approached Boaz.

Ruth's obedience to Naomi is endearing. She trusted Naomi more than anyone else and followed through with Naomi's plan because of that trust. We are not even sure if Ruth had any romantic inclination toward Boaz. We do know that being a widow in those days exposed a woman to much danger and made Ruth incredibly vulnerable. Naomi was seeking security for her dutiful and loyal daughter-in-law, and she was convinced that Boaz was the best husband choice for her. She had Ruth's best intentions at heart. The rest became history. Boaz took notice of Ruth, not because of her beauty, but because of her admirable character.

Ruth 2:11-12

And Boaz answered and said to her, "It has been fully reported to me, all that you have done for your mother-in-law since the death of your husband, and how you have left your father and your mother and the land of your birth, and have come to a people whom you did not know before. The Lord repay your work, and a full reward be given you by the Lord God of Israel, under whose wings you have come for refuge."

Based on the law of the land, the closest relative had the first right to take Ruth as his wife. Boaz, being a respectable man, wanted to do the right thing. When that relative rejected Ruth, Boaz married her instead. God then blessed them both with a child, whom they called Obed. He was the father of Jesse, who became the father of David. Jesus was born from their lineage—Jesus, our Redeemer, our Protector, and our Savior. We can see how Boaz's actions foreshadow what Jesus ultimately does for the whole world.

Throughout the Bible, we see previews of Christ. In the book of Ruth, Boaz is a "type" of Christ in that he "redeems" Ruth. Both Ruth and Naomi mention Boaz as a "kinsman." In Hebrew, the word is *"goel,"* which refers to a kinsman who has the "right to redeem" or a "redeemer." Throughout the Bible, that same Hebrew word is used several times. In the book of Job, Job declares, "I know that my Redeemer [goel] lives." While Boaz was a "kinsman redeemer," when Jesus came to Earth as a man, He became our "kinsman redeemer" in the flesh. Boaz redeemed Ruth, but years later Jesus would become the "redeemer" for the church, His bride. What a beautiful foreshadow!

Ruth received restoration, salvation, status, and was crafted into destiny. What about Naomi? In the height of her sorrow, she changed her name to Mara (meaning "bitter") and lamented over how she left Israel full and came home empty. However, because of her willingness to share her faith with a foreigner and her ability to nurture Ruth to follow after God, she ended up with a better destiny. Her shame was removed, and her status restored. What about you? Are there any "Ruths" in your life who God wants to graft into the kingdom and raise up to be mature daughters of the Most High? Would you be intentional to build that relationship with them to nurture them to fulfill their purpose?

The world may connect the word "mother" to a person who is fragile and fusses over the minutest things in life, but as God sees it, the woman who fully embraces her divine role of a kingdom mother holds the power to save a family and even a nation, if she wills.

Deborah

There came a time of turbulence and war in Israel where only a mother could deliver the nation from its destruction. Deborah, who we first mentioned in Chapter 3, was not known as a warrior; the Bible didn't emphasize her ability to prophesy, and she didn't deliver the nation because of her wisdom. God highlighted her motherhood as the reason for Israel's victory.

Judges 5:7

Village life ceased, it ceased in Israel,
Until I, Deborah, arose,
Arose a mother in Israel.

It was a time when women were regarded as property and had no rights; a time in history where women's voices were rarely heard. Despite the unfavorable environment, she arose. Who is the modern-day Deborah? She is a woman after God's heart. She will lead a generation to stand for God's ways of righteousness in the midst of a wicked and perverse generation. She carries the mother's heart to mentor, disciple, train, and nurture a generation that has suffered from rejection and lack of guidance. Will you arise and be that extension of God's maternal care to His people? Will you carry on the legacy of Deborah and be that mother to someone?

Eve The Last

Mother, motherhood, and mothering are defined in many ways in today's world, but the word *mother* encompasses a woman's eternal roles and her divine identity, and it describes her nature as a nurturer. With this perspective, the term *mother* is not restricted to a single act of giving physical life to a child but also to nurturing others. To nurture is to provide love and influence, to care for, support, educate, encourage, protect, and teach. To nurture is to help someone grow and develop.

God created Eve to carry the desire and ability to birth children, both naturally and spiritually, and to nurture them to maturity so they could accomplish their God-given purpose in life. God issued her the mandate to be fruitful and multiply and together with Adam to have dominion over creation and manifest the order of God's kingdom here on Earth. Henceforth, this is the same call for every woman after Eve. We can exercise our nature and nurture God's people toward maturity and health; to rally everyone in His family to showcase to the world what the kingdom of God is like. When unity is restored in the House of God, we will see the manifestation of God's power and glory on Earth.

Chapter 6

The Attack on Eve

God created Eden and it was bright and beautiful, but it was not perfect. It was completely good but not totally secured. We know this because Eden and her habitants were still vulnerable to the presence of evil in their midst, which was Satan. It was not a sanitized environment controlled by God. He gave the role of ruling and governing to Adam.

The Almighty created Eden with an abundance of good things, but it lacked the expansiveness that God so desired for His creation. Genesis 2:8 revealed a God who wished to see His creation multiplied and that men and women would have authority over every created thing. From the beginning, Eden was not meant to be static; it was destined for expansion. The devil, knowing that he was powerless to stop this expansion, purposed to disrupt and contaminate God's work; he chose to attack it through the weakest link.

Eve Was the Weaker Link

1 Peter 3:7

Husbands, likewise, dwell with them with understanding, giving honor to the wife, as to the weaker vessel, and as being heirs together of the grace of life, that your prayers may not be hindered.

Eve The Last

Peter, in one of his writings to the church, instructed husbands to honor their wives in spite of their wives being "weaker vessels." He warned them that failing to do so might hinder their prayers. In today's world, where equal rights are so widely fought for, to be considered the weaker sex seems demeaning. Yet, if we do not regard our Creator's Word and accept that the One who created us knows better, we become powerless to protect ourselves and unable to learn to defend our marriages and our territories. A woman's spirit may propel her to rise above the most traumatic events and sacrifice her life for the people she loves. However, she often finds herself depressed over matters of the heart: Self-doubt, insecurity, fears, and rejections plague her.

Eve was the weaker link; Satan knew that, and he came for her to launch his attack on humankind and their descendants. He came to bring chaos in the place of order. He came to break up covenant relationships so that God's power and blessings could not come to the people and through the people. Without the power of God, humans would not be able to effectively bring about God's dominion on the Earth. Satan saw an open door through Eve and came to deceive her. William James, an American philosopher and psychologist and a leading thinker in the eighteenth century, reflected on this: *"A chain is no stronger than its weakest link, and life is after all a chain."* Satan came that day with the most devious scheme to cause Adam and Eve to break their covenant relationships with God and with each other, and the same is true for us today. It was in the Garden of Eden that man hailed the first accusation. Through his words, Adam separated himself from Eve, which became the first crack that led to many fractures in relationships thereafter.

Genesis 3:12

Then the man said, "The woman whom You gave to be with me, she gave me of the tree, and I ate."

106

Imagine Eve standing there listening to Adam as he chose to separate himself from her and push her back onto God! Apparently, Adam had forgotten what he said in Genesis 2:23 when he (regarding Eve) exclaimed, *"This is now bone of my bones and flesh of my flesh; She shall be called Woman, because she was taken out of Man."* This distinction marked the beginning of Eve's (and thereafter, all women's) struggle with her self-worth. She was made for Adam but rejected in this instance. I can imagine Eve's world was plunged into internal chaos. Adam, being her covering, did not choose to cover her (1 Cor. 11)!

When sin and self-seeking enter the heart of man, the relationship takes on a different dimension that God never intended. The once harmonious relationship that is demonstrated by a sense of oneness and the balance of power given to each other is now bombarded by the need to seek love and power within a relationship. Now, the balance of power and the giving of love in a marriage becomes the point of contention and strife.

Genesis 3:16

To the woman He said: "I will greatly multiply your sorrow and your conception; In pain you shall bring forth children; Your desire shall be for your husband, and he shall rule over you."

Eve was the weaker link. God knew it, but He did not stop Satan from his actions. It is important for us to understand that God would not take over the responsibilities He had given to man in the garden. He would not violate the free will of man even though He knew Adam would mess up. At the same time, in His grace, God made a path of redemption. Remember, our God is all-knowing and all-powerful. We can't hide anything from Him, and nothing can stand in His way to accomplish His purpose. He is our redeemer!

E^{The Last}ve

God's Plan for Eve

Revelation 1:8

"I am the Alpha and the Omega," says the Lord God, "who is and who was and who is to come, the Almighty."

God is the original author of the story of mankind. He started the story, and He will be the one to end it. The book of Revelation shows us that the end will be glorious. Christ will come back for the church and He will return to see her in glory and power. However, before this happens, He must allow His creation to develop the content of the story that He is writing. He will painstakingly allow man to make mistakes and suffer the consequences of his actions to learn self-control. He will sometimes lift up His protective hands so that man can learn how to fight the darkness coming against him and reclaim his children from rebellion or save a spouse going down the pit of alcoholism. Some people believe that if God is good then this means that nothing bad should happen to them if they walk with Him. When something bad happens, it implies that they have sinned against God.

This is a wrong and dangerous theology. Though it may seem true in some instances, we must understand that God's goodness cannot be defined by our lack of troubles. We live in a broken-down world and are equally exposed to its repercussions. However, God loves His people and in His covenant with us, He promises His protection. Yet, at the same time, He desires for us to not be weak in our faith and to develop our spiritual maturity. As such, He bases His decision to protect us or to allow us to go through fire on what will benefit us. This is the overall purpose He has for us and for the church at large. Nevertheless, the Bible tells us that He will never allow us to go through more than we can bear. Furthermore, He assures us that if we have to go through the fire, He will never leave nor forsake us but will be with us, as He was the fourth man in the fire with Shadrach, Meshach, and Abednego (Dan. 3)!

1 Corinthians 10:13 (MSG)

No test or temptation that comes your way is beyond the course of what others have had to face. All you need to remember is that God will never let you down; he'll never let you be pushed past your limit; he'll always be there to help you come through it.

God did not stop Satan. He did not step into the role that Adam should. He let the events unfold. But He sought out Adam and Eve even though they had disobeyed Him. He came to demonstrate this truth: That no matter the failure, He is a good Father and will seek him out and desire to restore the relationship. Although Adam sinned and broke the commandment of the Father, He still came into the garden to bring order and did not cut off relationship with Adam and Eve.

Genesis 3:21

Also, for Adam and his wife the Lord God made tunics of skin and clothed them.

God doesn't intervene in what man is responsible to do. God will not interfere and expects him to do what is right. However, if man fails or rebels, God will then intervene to set things in order. That day, Eve understood that despite her mistake, her Creator still loved her and would protect her. Her identity did not stem from Adam but from the Maker of heaven and Earth. Her worth was found not in the things she could do but in the One who made her. Her destiny was not determined by Adam's recognition but by Her Father's intention. Eve was the weaker vessel, but God lent His strength and trained her hands for battle. She will carry Him within her and will not fail in her assignment, especially in the end-times.

Psalm 46:5

God is in her. She will not fall. God will help her at daybreak.

Training Her Hands for Battle

Psalm 144:1

Blessed be the Lord my Rock,
who trains my hands for battle,
my fingers for war.

Much betrayal, injustice, and accusations plagued David's life. Despite all his challenges, he recognized that God was training him to grow from a passionate lad to a spiritual giant. God desires to train us, His people, because we live in a dimension that is hostile to faith, hope, and love. Spiritual terrorists seek to engulf our righteousness and contaminate our holiness. We must learn from the Holy Spirit how to fight against principalities, powers, and rulers who set out to divide and conquer the kingdom of righteousness.

Ephesians 6:12

For we do not wrestle against flesh and blood, but against principalities, against powers, against the rulers of the darkness of this age, against spiritual hosts of wickedness in the heavenly places.

Through their subtle influences, demons work their way into churches, families, and societies by hurting people who are ignorant of their existence. Yes, God has to train His people to push back darkness, to close the doors that need to be shut, and to open the doors that need to be opened.

Revelation 3:7-9

"And to the angel of the church in Philadelphia write, 'These things says He who is holy, He who is true, "He who has the key of David, He who opens and no one shuts, and shuts and no one opens": "I know your works. See, I have set before you an open door, and no one can shut it; for you have a little strength, have kept My word, and have not denied My name. Indeed I will make those of the synagogue of Satan, who say they are Jews and are not, but lie—indeed I will make them come and worship before your feet, and to know that I have loved you."

Eve was the weaker vessel. Satan knew it. God knew it, and He needed Eve to know it. God did not create Eve to be invincible but to be vulnerable. Her vulnerability was her strength, yet when untrained it would also be her weakness and downfall. Revelation 3 records the letter the apostle John wrote to the church in Philadelphia. It is also a present revelation for the churches today that purpose to keep the Word of God despite social and moral degradation. It is also symbolically relevant to every woman who desires to know how to shut the door to darkness and open the door for the light of God to shine through her life.

> **God did not create Eve to be invincible but to be vulnerable.**

Every woman mentioned in the Bible symbolizes the Church. Ephesians 5 instructs husbands to love their wives just as Christ also loves the Church and gave Himself for Her, making a parallel comparison of women to that of the Church. Scripture further describes the

Eve The Last

Lord's desire to sanctify and cleanse Her with the washing of water by the Word, with the intention to present Her to Himself a glorious Church, not having spot or wrinkle or any such thing, but that she should be holy and without blemish. At this, the Word once again directs husbands, reminding them that they ought to love their own wives as their own bodies; he who loves his wife loves himself. For no one ever hated his own flesh, but nourishes and cherishes it, just as the Lord does the Church. God is determined to bring the Church to a place of glory.

As every woman is a representation of the Church, likewise, God is steadfast to train the hands of every woman who is willing and obedient. He will show us the key of David and train us to shut the door from demons and open the door for the power of the Spirit of God to come through us! If women symbolize the Church, then men symbolize Christ, the head. Men have the same assignment to come alongside Christ to cover and heal the women in their lives, to become undefiled by the world, and to be the gateway for the influence of His holiness and righteousness.

The Three Battlegrounds of a Woman: Heart, Mind, Voice

(A) Her Heart

Proverbs 4:23 (CSB)

Guard your heart above all else, for it is the source of life.

The New Living Translation added that we must guard our heart, above all else, for it determines the course of our lives. The Bible is clear when stating that the condition of our hearts will affect our choices and our choices will lead us to where we end up in life.

An example of a nuclear submarine provides an excellent picture of our hearts. Nuclear submarines consist of some of the most amazing technology on the planet. These incredible military vessels can stay underwater for ninety days, but every ninety days the submarine must resurface to maintain proper alignment with the North Star. While underwater, Earth's magnetic forces affect the submarine's navigational system. Hence, through time Earth will move out of alignment with the North Star; because these submarines carry missiles of mass destruction, it would be disastrous if they missed their targets by even a hairline! Though the submarine may have enough physical provisions, like food, water, or fuel, it cannot perform at its highest level or complete its mission without maintaining proper alignment with the true reference point.

Your heart is the navigational equipment of your life. It must stay aligned with God. By guarding your heart, you stay locked into God's will and the "source of life." A woman who wants to experience the fullness of her faith and partake of God's blessings must recognize that her heart is her power source. "Above all else" communicates priority and identifies guarding your heart as more important than anything else.

To the Christian community that cherishes the doctrine of self-denial as one of the key aspects of following Christ, guarding your heart appears to be a contradiction. Are we expected to "take up our cross" and not take care of our hearts? I am convinced that Proverbs 4:23-27 contains another great paradox of kingdom living. Could it be that we can only die to self when we guard our hearts?

Look at what the Bible says about the role of the heart. Jesus declared that we should love the Lord our God with all our heart, soul, mind, and strength (Mark 12:30). When describing the kingdom of God, Jesus revealed the things that come out of the heart that defile a man (Matt.

15:16-20). He also taught, *"For where your treasure is, there your heart will be also"* (Luke 12:34). The apostle Paul prayed for the saints that *"the eyes of your heart may be enlightened"* (Eph. 1:18). We find similar instruction in the Old Testament where we are commanded to trust the Lord with all our heart (Prov. 3:5) and to hide God's Word in our heart (Ps. 119:11). The prophet Samuel revealed that God does not evaluate people by outward appearance, but He looks at the heart (1 Sam. 16:7). Perhaps the most significant verse describing the treasure of the heart appears in Romans 10:9, which says a person will be saved by "believing in your heart" that God raised Jesus from the dead.

What Is the Heart?

The heart is the organ that distinguishes the living from the dead. What is true in the natural is also true in the spirit. The spiritual heart is the place in our inner being where our intellect, emotions, and will intersect to make decisions. In this place, we form the perception of what is good and bad and right and wrong.

Woody Allen

Back in the 1990s, the comedian and filmmaker Woody Allen was a movie-industry icon—that is until his personal life began to unravel. His long-term affair with Mia Farrow came to an ugly end just after they had a child together. A short time later, it was discovered that Allen was romantically involved with Mia's seventeen-year-old adopted daughter, Soon-Yi. The inappropriateness of that relationship scandalized even the most jaded Hollywood observers, but Allen seemed to find nothing wrong with dating the teenaged daughter of his former girlfriend. When a reporter challenged him on the matter, Allen rationalized and defended his actions, then concluded the discussion by declaring, *"The heart wants what it wants."* He seemed to be paraphrasing the late philosopher Pascal, who said, *"The heart has reasons that reason does not know."*

"The heart wants what it wants." As disturbing as that defense was, it reflects a truth that the heart is the control center of a person's life. Unlike robots that can be programmed to function in certain ways or animals who can be trained to behave properly, who we are and what we do is ultimately determined by the condition of our hearts. We are human beings who think, feel, and choose, and the place where our thoughts, emotions, and will intersect is right here, at the center of our beings—the heart. In the end, our hearts will reveal who we are, and in any given situation, our hearts will determine what we do. Dr. Charles Ryrie defined the heart as "the very core of life." Our hearts are the truest expression of who we really are.

Proverbs 27:19

As in water face reflects face,
So, a man's heart reveals the man.

The heart is more than our minds, emotions, and choices. It is where all of these things come together to shape our lives and faith. So, we can understand why it's so important for our hearts to be pure.

This is why Jesus says, *"Blessed are the pure in heart, for they shall see God"* (Matt. 5:8).

Psalm 24:3-5

Who may ascend into the hill of the Lord?
Or who may stand in His holy place?
He who has clean hands and a pure heart,
Who has not lifted up his soul to an idol,

E_{The Last}ve

Nor sworn deceitfully.
He shall receive blessing from the Lord,
And righteousness from the God of his salvation.

A woman's heart is her most violently fought battleground.

Having identified the biblical mandate for us to recognize the treasure of the heart, we must prioritize the task of guarding our hearts. The heart is a mysterious spiritual reality that allows us to experience the fullness of life. According to Scripture, the heart can be grieved, troubled, broken, pierced, divided, and sometimes can stop beating entirely! In John 7, Jesus announced to his disciples about the coming of the Holy Spirit and likened the Spirit of God to rivers of living water. This water will flow from our hearts, and where the river flows it will spring forth life—the kind of life that comes from God—full of vitality and power.

John 7:37-39

On the last day, that great day of the feast, Jesus stood and cried out, saying, "If anyone thirsts, let him come to Me and drink. He who believes in Me, as the Scripture has said, **out of his heart will flow rivers of living water.***" But this He spoke concerning the Spirit, whom those believing in Him would receive; for the Holy Spirit was not yet given, because Jesus was not yet glorified.*

However, when the life source is contaminated, the life that flows out of it will lose its flavor and, in some cases, bring about destruction instead of life. This is why a woman's heart is her most violently fought battleground. Satan will spare no effort at breaking her heart to strip her of her needed power source to accomplish her assignment.

Betrayal, accusations, injustice, fear, and bitter envy are common arsenals from the enemy grounds. They target women's hearts to divert them away from fighting for God to fighting against people and men, especially. When we do not know how to deal with these attacks (instead of acknowledging the situation and finding healing from the Word and yielding to the Spirit) we tend to push our pain away and deny its effects; when we do, this clogs our hearts and causes them to shut down! Many Christians, if not most, are walking around with a hardened, shutdown heart. Much like what happens to a physical heart, the spiritual heart cannot function when it's clogged.

Do you know what happens to a person when their physical heart gets clogged and hardens? Eventually, they die from this condition, and a hardened spiritual heart will do the exact same thing to them. Many women, like Eve in the garden, have had their hearts broken by people and situations. The solution is never to be isolated from relationships and emotions; that is denying the way God designed you to function. We relate in the kingdom of God through relationships that build one another up and this, in effect, will move the kingdom from glory to glory. The heart holds the most important role of connecting the body of Christ together. No wonder the devil will attack the heart first by breaking it and filling it with darkness!

Dangers of a Shutdown Heart

Growing up, Diana (not her real name) did not receive the care that she needed. She was sexually violated and exposed to things a young child should never see or participate in. Not knowing how to cope with the trauma and violence, she had learned to shut down her heart so that she could continue to function. She thought she had found love when she met her husband in her young age, but he turned out to be an adulterer who knew nothing about being faithful. The infidelity caused Diana's heart to descend into a major lockdown.

When her baby girl Tricia came along, Diana found herself ill-equipped to show love to her and communicate with her. The older Tricia grew, the further mother and daughter grew apart. Diana tried to be a good mother and provided everything that Tricia needed except the most important thing: the connection with her mother. Diana started to understand the effects of her own shutdown heart on her daughter when Tricia began having trouble building healthy relationships with her school and church friends. She felt that she didn't "belong"; she battled a sense of isolation and hopelessness. Diana understood then how the condition of her heart directly impacted her daughter and decided to seek help for her own issues. Today, Diana is on her path to taking back the power of her heart and allowing God to heal her and her daughter. She now understands that her shutdown heart not only cripples relationships with people she cares about but is also a curse that will harm the next generation.

In Luke 8, the Lord was trying to explain to His followers the mysteries of God's kingdom realm. To help them understand, He used the parable of a farmer who sowed seeds to reap a harvest. The seeds fell into four types of grounds: hard pathway, gravel ground, thorny ground, and, finally, the fertile soil. Of course, the first three types of ground did not yield any harvest. The fertile soil, however, produced a harvest. We understand that Jesus was comparing the heart of a man to that of fertile soil, and we can see that He was determined to make them understand the importance of an open heart. Jesus ended His parable, shouting out to all who would hear, *"Listen with your heart and you will understand!"*

You see, we hear with our ears but understand with our hearts. If our hearts are shut, we can't comprehend and receive truth; therefore, we will not be able to "see" God's kingdom and walk in the power of it here on Earth. The disciples, apparently not understanding what Jesus was trying to convey, asked Him privately what deeper meaning was found in this parable. With that, Jesus began to expound on the importance of a heart that is teachable as it is the heart that allows us to listen to, see, and understand spiritual truths.

Luke 8:10 (TPT)

He said, "You have been given a teachable heart to perceive the secret, hidden mysteries of God's kingdom realm. But to those who don't have a listening heart, my words are merely stories. Even though they have eyes, they are blind to the true meaning of what I say, and even though they listen, they won't receive full revelation."

He continued in verses 11 to 15, explaining that the condition of our hearts will determine the degree to which we receive truth and produce the change we want to see. In conclusion, we need to have the heart that represents the fertile soil.

Luke 8:15 (TPT)

The seed that fell into good, fertile soil represents those lovers of truth who hear it deep within their hearts. They respond by clinging to the word, keeping it dear as they endure all things in faith. This is the seed that will one day bear much fruit in their lives.

As Luke 8:10 and 8:15 show, a hardened heart dulls the ability to understand Truth. A person with a hardened heart puts up walls, which disables them from receiving anything. Not only that, but darkness takes residence, meaning there is no room for revelation-light to enter. Jesus, three chapters later, responded to the crowd that asked for a sign that He was the Messiah:

Eve The Last

Luke 11:34-35 (TPT)

The eyes of your spirit allow revelation-light to enter into your being. When your heart is open the light floods in. When your heart is hard and closed, the light cannot penetrate, and darkness takes its place. Open your heart and consider my words. Watch out that you do not mistake your opinions for revelation-light!

"*Watch out that you do not mistake your opinions for revelation-light!*" A heart that is shut down runs the danger of misinterpreting the Word of God and the heart of God! After all, we do interpret the words according to the conditions of our hearts. We need to take heed to keep our hearts pure, just as instructed by the Lord, so that we can truly see God and what He wants to do with twenty-twenty vision!

If your heart is hardened, not only are you blind, but you can't hear and darkness overcomes you. Demons will try to torment and deceive you.

(B) Her Mind

Romans 12:2 (TPT)

Stop imitating the ideals and opinions of the culture around you but be inwardly transformed by the Holy Spirit through a total reformation of how you think. This will empower you to discern God's will as you live a beautiful life, satisfying and perfect in his eyes.

Romans 12:2 shows us that a life aligned with God's will is beautiful, satisfying, and perfect. We come into this life by allowing the Holy Spirit to reform our thinking to that of a kingdom perspective. Jesus taught kingdom principles that challenge our thinking about worldly ideals and opinions. This Scripture also shows us that our thinking holds the power to determine how we behave. If we think as the world does, we will imitate the world, but when we align our thinking with the Word of God, we will imitate the culture of God's kingdom. Jesus said that God's kingdom cannot be seen with natural eyes; it must be seen with the eyes of our hearts.

We must allow the Holy Spirit to do deep, transformative work in our hearts before our minds can be reformed to the ways of the kingdom of God. Romans 8:27 says that the Holy Spirit knows the mind of God and makes intercession on our behalf in accordance with God's will. The Holy Spirit will reveal the things in our hearts that are not in alignment with God's will because He purposes to purify our hearts. Your heart is the entry point to your mind. To the pure at heart, all things are pure. Thus, as the heart becomes pure, so does the mind. Purity of heart and mind will empower you to not be so easily disturbed or tempted. However, when our hearts are not right, this gives way for demons to infiltrate our minds!

Joyce Meyer, well-known author of *Battlefield of the Mind*, wrote: "A war is raging, and your mind is the battlefield. If you've ever dealt with things like worry, doubt, confusion, depression, anger, condemnation … you've experienced firsthand the attacks in your mind."

Satan uses this weapon against women, as he did to Eve. He sowed a contradicting thought into Eve's mind, challenging the Word of God. He cast doubt in her mind to think that she had mistaken what God was saying—the Bible said she was deceived (2 Cor. 11:3). Eve was naïve, did not perceive evil speaking to her, and chose to entertain the second voice.

Purity of heart and mind is innocence, not naiveté. A person fully endowed with purity of heart and mind knows God's Word and trusts His character. Naiveté is the opposite of innocence—it is ignorance of truth and leads to a corrupt type of influence that controls and manipulates an individual. A great example of innocence as a strength appears in Luke 18:16-17, where Jesus likens innocence to the posture of a child. In fact, He says this posture of innocence is the means by which a person experiences the fullness of God's kingdom.

Luke 18:16-17

But Jesus called them to Him and said, "Let the little children come to Me, and do not forbid them; for of such is the kingdom of God. Assuredly, I say to you, whoever does not receive the kingdom of God as a little child will by no means enter it."

Jesus says you must receive the kingdom of God with innocence, like a child whose heart and mind are pure. Often, we as adults have life experiences that harden our hearts and cause our minds to question and distrust, making it impossible to see God's kingdom. Have you ever noticed how children, by nature, are often too easily trusting of others and not suspicious of a person's intentions? Instead, they explore their world with exciting imagination and curiosity! For this reason, Jesus said you, too, must approach the kingdom of God with purity of heart and mind, easily trusting the character of God, alert and aware of His goodness and truth! In the world, this is perceived as being naïve, and, of course, God does not want us to be childlike in immaturity; He wants us to have childlike innocence.

You do not have to return to the age of a child to have your heart and mind reformed to innocence. You begin by heeding God. His must be the first and most prominent voice in your life, without which the devil will constantly torment you. In fact, the book of James teaches that we can resist the devil by submitting to God and allowing His Word to purify our hearts! The Bible says that a double-minded man will receive nothing from the Lord (James 1:7-8). Who is a double-minded man? It is one whose mind is formed according to both the world and the Word of God. King David, in Psalm 119:113, exclaimed that he hates the double-minded but loves God's law, which is the Word of God. I believe that to be single-minded, we must first love the Word of God in our hearts and this will transform our thinking.

The great thinker William James says, *"The greatest weapon against stress is our ability to choose one thought over another."* Just as 2 Corinthians 10:5 says, *"Bringing every thought into captivity to the obedience of Christ."* When the Word of God purifies your heart, you can discern the source of your thinking and be empowered to do away with thoughts that don't sync with God's Word. Satan gains access through our insecure hearts, causes us to constantly doubt our self-worth, and steals our confidence. Most women struggle with stress, fear, and anxiety. As women, we hold many responsibilities and often make great multitaskers, but we are quick to criticize ourselves; and if anything goes wrong, we are quick to take the blame. The feeling of not being good enough is our constant companion. Satan is quick to remind us of why we should not venture into business. He paints a picture of how embarrassed we would be if we said the wrong thing in front of people. He questions our ability to lead others and casts doubt about whether we can truly make a difference in the lives of those we lead. These voices in our heads do not come from God; they come from the pit of hell to disturb, distract, and destroy us. When we listen to them, we become confused and weakened in our resolve to believe and trust what God is saying to us. We become emotionally drained and frustrated with

An ungodly belief is anything you believe that is not in agreement with God's Word, nature, or character.

ourselves, our situations, and our relationships. Furthermore, when we agree with these voices, we bind ourselves with ungodly beliefs.

An ungodly belief is anything you believe that is not in agreement with God's Word, nature, or character. Often, it is caused by people speaking negative things to you or about you, or by painful experiences. These false belief systems restrict you in life, in your faith, and in your relationship with God and other people. They make you see your situation through tainted glass and distort your view of God and others. What is most destructive is that ungodly beliefs are covenants with the enemy and must therefore be broken.

Proverbs 23:7

For as he thinks in his heart, so is he …

What you think in your heart, you become. No wonder God's Word instructs us to put on the mind of Christ. Philippians 2:5 tells us to allow the same mind that was in Christ to be in us. If we have the mind of Christ, then we will be Christlike. Eve entertained a second voice, and this caused her to lose her grip on God's instruction through Adam. Let us reverse this and reinstate the status of God's voice in our lives. Let us train our hearts to hear from the Holy Spirit and yield ourselves to obey the Word. When God's voice gets louder, the voice of demons will flee. Hearing the voice of God is not rocket science, but it does start with a decision to do so. You must understand that God wants to speak to you, and, in fact, He is speaking to you right now. You may not be hearing His voice or sensing His presence because of a clogged-up heart and because your mind has been filled with other voices.

Galatians 5:17

For the flesh lusts against the Spirit, and the Spirit against the flesh; and these are contrary to one another, so that you do not do the things that you wish.

Our flesh is in constant war with our spirits. Who you listen to will be the voice of influence in your life. When you yield to these voices, you come into agreement with them, and now what they say will become what you say.

(C) Her Voice

Galatians 6:8

For he who sows to his flesh will of the flesh reap corruption, but he who sows to the Spirit will of the Spirit reap everlasting life.

Our voice is a weapon. What we say holds tremendous power to build up or tear down! With our natural ability to speak and communicate, this can be a major threat against the power of darkness or it can destroy our own lives! This is why Satan wants to corrupt our words to his advantage. The Bible is clear that defilement comes not from what goes in the mouth but from what comes out of the mouth (Matt. 15:11).

> **Our voice is a weapon. What we say holds tremendous power to build up or tear down!**

Proverbs 18:21

Death and life are in the power of the tongue, and those who love it will eat its fruit.

Your words can bring life to the situation (or even your heart!) that is dead or can put to death something that is living. Ephesians 6 talks about the armor of spiritual warfare. Paul charged the church to be strong in the Lord and in the power of His might, and you do so by putting on the whole armor of God!

Ephesians 6:10-18

Finally, my brethren, be strong in the Lord and in the power of His might. Put on the whole armor of God, that you may be able to stand against the wiles of the devil. For we do not wrestle against flesh and blood, but against principalities, against powers, against the rulers of the darkness of this age, against spiritual hosts of wickedness in the heavenly places. Therefore take up the whole armor of God, that you may be able to withstand in the evil day, and having done all, to stand. Stand therefore, having girded your waist with truth, having put on the breastplate of righteousness, and having shod your feet with the preparation of the gospel of peace; above all, taking the shield of faith with which you will be able to quench all the fiery darts of the wicked one. And take the helmet of salvation, and the sword of the Spirit, which is the word of God; praying always with all prayer and supplication in the Spirit, being watchful to this end with all perseverance and supplication for all the saints.

The passage described six pieces of armor that God has prepared for us:

(i)   Girdle of Truth

(ii)   Breastplate of Righteousness

(iii) Shoes of the Gospel of Peace

(iv)   Shield of Faith

(v)   Helmet of Salvation

(vi)   Sword of the Spirit

The first five pieces are all *defensive* armor. Truth, righteousness, peace, faith, and salvation (sound mind) help us "withstand" the forces of darkness in the evil day. However, the last piece of the armor—the sword of the Spirit, which represents the Word of God—is the only *offensive* weapon. As believers, we are called to advance the kingdom of God, to bring light into the places of darkness. Hence, we need to fully endow ourselves with the whole armor and learn to use the sword of the Spirit to take ground. But take note: We use the sword effectively through our prayers—the words from our mouths!

2 Corinthians 6:11-13 (MSG)

Dear, dear Corinthians, I can't tell you how much I long for you to enter this wide-open, spacious life. We didn't fence you in. The smallness you feel comes from within you. Your lives aren't small, but you're living them in a small way. I'm speaking as plainly as I can and with great affection. Open up your lives. Live openly and expansively!

Our God is one of expansion, not preservation. He desires for you to live openly and expansively. He wants you to grow in your abilities, gifts, and talents to be effective at home, in the workplace, and in church. He desires to see His people growing in their influence and authority both naturally and spiritually. In Isaiah 54:2, He challenges us: *"Do not spare; lengthen your cords and strengthen your stakes."* God's heart wants us to keep expanding our territory of influence and authority (Mark 4:30-32). To do that, we need to use the only offensive weapon we have: the Word of God. The sword does no damage to the territory of darkness if it remains in our hands. However, when we speak it out, we push back demons and the kingdom of God advances. In addressing Peter, Jesus said, *"On this rock I will build My church, and the gates of Hades shall not prevail against it. And I will give you the keys of the kingdom of heaven, and whatever you bind on earth will be bound in heaven, and whatever you loose on earth will be loosed in heaven"* (Matt. 16:18-20). The power of Hades will not have power to come against the church, but the church can only advance if we are wise in using our prayers to bind what needs to be bound and release what needs to be released.

God made Eve to be communicative. He designed her with the ability to speak so that she could agree with Him to manifest His kingdom. When we agree with God, power is released through our confession to heal hearts, to lift up blind eyes, to build faith, to establish order, to destroy the violation of demons, and establish righteousness, peace, and joy.

Romans 14:17

For the kingdom of God is not eating and drinking, but righteousness and peace and joy in the Holy Spirit.

When we use our voices as God intended, we can manifest the reality of His kingdom. This kingdom is more than speaking in tongues, casting out demons, or performing miracles, signs, and wonders! It reflects a way of life, a demonstration of the kinds of relationships that please God, and it establishes an order where authority, anointing, and blessing flow from one to another.

However, when your heart is wounded and your mind is given to darkness, your words will have no power (even though they may sound right). When provoked, your words may even carry death and destroy relationships, especially covenanted ones. Instead of bringing order, we create disorder through our gossip and conspiracy. We stir up guilt and condemnation through our wrongful accusations. We release missiles of destruction into home ground instead of enemy ground, paving the way for demons to accentuate their influence and multiply their effects. Before we know it, the walls that protect the kingdom are shattered and no one is protected. Instead, Satan and his army ravage the people of God and cause them to fornicate with the world; blinded and wounded, we can no long differentiate what is right from wrong.

Like Eve, we have a passion to please God and be a blessing to the ones we are called to, but we live in a broken-down world, where Satan is waiting to devour us. To navigate safely and still fulfill our destiny, we must know the identity of our enemy and what we need to do to advance our influence and take authority over the sphere God has willed for us. Satan has one objective: to contaminate everything that God loves. He does that through principalities, powers, and rulers of darkness that come against God's people. Through the Jezebel spirit, Satan seeks to destroy our relationships and promote fear and mistrust. But God, through the work of the Holy Spirit, will raise up an army of *Deborahs* who will bring order and restore the headship of man.

Chapter 7

The Jezebel, Leviathan, and Absalom Influence

In this book, we have concluded that a hardened heart is dangerous because it will cause you to lose your source of power and open you up to torment and deception. In addition, it will distort and contaminate the things that leave your mouth. By far, what is the most dangerous consequence of a hardened heart? A hardened heart left unchecked will become a place for the powers of darkness to operate and create chaos. This stronghold brings about destruction in relationships and causes spiritual death and sometimes physical death.

In this chapter, I want to help you understand the dark forces that have been unleashed against the people of God, especially against the women of God. Fighting spiritual warfare is not a matter of choice. Satan is set on destroying God's people. If you do not fight, you are already a casualty, but if you do fight, you will have victory because God fights along with you! The Bible says in Psalm 46:5 (NIV) that *"God is*

Fighting spiritual warfare is not a matter of choice.

within her; she will not fall; God will help her at break of day." By putting on the armor of God, using our prayer language and the Word of God, we can withstand the evil one! We will surely win! Jesus has overcome the cross, death, and Satan himself! And as He is, so are we! To succeed in a battle, we need to know our authority and understand our enemies' strategies.

"If you know the enemy and know yourself, you need not fear the result of a hundred battles. If you know yourself but not the enemy, for every victory gained you will also suffer a defeat. If you know neither the enemy nor yourself, you will succumb in every battle."

~ Sun Tzu, The Art of War

Jezebel is a territorial (principality) spirit that does not inhabit a body. Ephesians 6:12 instructs us about the spiritual forces of evil in the heavenly realms; Jezebel is one of these, along with Leviathan and others. Jezebel directs earthly demons to damage and destroy God's people.

Operation of the Jezebel Spirit

Revelation 2:20

Nevertheless, I have a few things against you, because you allow that woman Jezebel, who calls herself a prophetess, to teach and seduce My servants to commit sexual immorality and eat things sacrificed to idols.

Understand that this spirit existed long before it got its name. The Bible refers to it as a "she"; however it is without gender. Jezebel was referred to as a person in the Old Testament but as a spirit in the New

Testament. It was conferred the name "Jezebel" because the epitome of the spirit's destructive effect was demonstrated through the historical woman Jezebel found in 1 Kings 16. She was introduced as the rebellious, manipulative wife of King Ahab. This spirit that operated through Queen Jezebel caused over ten million (all but seven thousand) Hebrews to succumb to bowing to Baal. Through Jezebel's influence, the people forsook their covenant with Jehovah and were steeped into idolatry. Jezebel destroyed the sacred altars and killed the prophets who refused to submit to her. This spirit was entirely responsible for corrupting a whole nation. The Jezebel spirit is not a mere demon but a principality who targets particular people (and nations) of God.

1 Kings 18:4

For so it was, while Jezebel massacred the prophets of the Lord, that Obadiah had taken one hundred prophets and hidden them, fifty to a cave, and had fed them with bread and water.

In his book *The Jezebel Spirit,* Francis Frangipane gives great insight into this spirit and the way it operates. I encourage you to read his book to gain a better perspective on this subject and develop your discernment of how to deal with this spirit and its influence on you and others around you. Frangipane wrote in his blog, *"It is important to note that, while men in leadership are the main targets of most principalities, Jezebel is more attracted to the uniqueness of the female psyche in its sophisticated ability to manipulate without physical force."*

This spirit targets women who are embittered against men because of neglect or misuse of authority. It rides on women who, because of insecurity or jealousy or vanity, desire to dominate others. Oftentimes, the woman who exhibits the Jezebelic influence will be seen publicly putting her husband down with her words and attempting to control him through his fear of public embarrassment. An example would be Michal, King David's wife. Michal used to be a woman full of love for David; however, betrayed and abandoned by the men in her life, she gave into the influence of demons. When she saw King David take off his kingly robe, leaping and dancing before the Lord, she despised him in her heart. "Despised" in Hebrew is a very, very strong word. She had absolutely no respect or reverence for him. A feeling of hate and bitterness rose up in her heart against him and everything that he stood for. And from her mouth came judgment, anger, and hatred.

2 Samuel 6:20

Then David returned to bless his household. And Michal the daughter of Saul came out to meet David, and said, "How glorious was the king of Israel today, uncovering himself today in the eyes of the maids of his servants, as one of the base fellows shamelessly uncovers himself!"

Her words of gross disrespect broke their relationship, and the Bible says that Michal was barren until the day she died. When a woman's heart is hardened, she cannot have God's values of a marriage. A woman with an unhealed heart will find no place to love and submit. The name "Jezebel," literally translated, means "without cohabitation." Jezebel will not submit herself to anyone unless it is for a strategic reason and her own advantage. Frangipane says, "From her heart, she yields to no one."

First Kings 21 records a story of a vineyard owner, Naboth, whose refusal to sell his land to King Ahab greatly upset the king. Since Naboth inherited the land from his ancestors, the Mosaic law forbade the sale. When King Ahab's wife, Queen Jezebel, learned why Ahab was unhappy, she decided to take matters into her own hands. She usurped the king's authority, forged his signature, and set Naboth up for death. She declared a fast and planted two scoundrels to sit with Naboth and falsely accuse him of cursing God and the king. Afterward, they took Naboth outside the city and stoned him to death. After Naboth's execution, the Queen told Ahab to take possession of the vineyard. On the surface, it would seem like Jezebel was for the king, yet everything she did, she did to satisfy his carnality so that she could continue to control him.

1 Kings 21:7

Then Jezebel his wife said to him, "You now exercise authority over Israel! Arise, eat food, and let your heart be cheerful; I will give you the vineyard of Naboth the Jezreelite."

It is very clear who wears the pants in this relationship. For a Jezebel to reign, there must exist an Ahab who is willing to be the puppet in her hands. In relationships where the Jezebelic influence is present, you often see the reversal of roles—the woman assuming the headship while the man is usually pushed back and emasculated. Through her leadership, Jezebel stirred up Ahab to sin against God and abandon his spiritual heritage.

1 Kings 21:25

But there was no one like Ahab who sold himself to do wickedness in the sight of the Lord, because Jezebel his wife stirred him up.

The spirit of Jezebel also seeks to control her prey by means of sexual perversions. She influences women to use their sexuality to control men. When overcome, the victim loses his ability to break away despite knowing that something is amiss. This kind of spirit seduces men to destroy their ability to lead and fulfill their God-given assignment. Stirring up lust within her prey, this spirit corrupts his mind and often causes him to lose sight of his present dangers and vision of his future destiny. We see a good example of this dynamic in the story of Samson and Delilah.

Proverbs 7:21-23

With her enticing speech she caused him to yield,
With her flattering lips she seduced him.
Immediately he went after her, as an ox goes to the slaughter,
Or as a fool to the correction of the stocks,
Till an arrow struck his liver.
As a bird hastens to the snare,
He did not know it would cost his life.

Samson, a God-appointed Nazirite who possessed great physical strength and served as the final judge of Israel, was brought down by a mere woman. The Bible does not clarify whether Delilah was extremely beautiful or if she had any extraordinary skills. Though clearly Samson struggled with a lust for women, he was able to "run away" from them when he needed to. He left his wife from Timnah because he was upset with her. He ran away from the prostitute in Gaza when his enemies came to ambush him. But not so with Delilah; Samson could not leave her, even though he knew she didn't love him the same way he loved her. Despite the Philistines ambushing him twice, he did not perceive the danger with Delilah and escape before being captured and destroyed. Many credited that to him being overly confident and extremely arrogant. However, I believe the spirit of Jezebel was working through Delilah, which is why she had Samson bound in the first place. Strong as he was, he could not withstand her constant, spiritual torment. The Bible says her constant pestering vexed him to death, and therefore he gave up the secret of his strength. Samson then lost his power, and the enemies overcame him. As mentioned earlier, the Philistines gorged his eyes out while he was in chains. I believe this symbolizes the fact that a man (or a woman) under the influence of seduction loses sight of where they are and spiritual vision about where they are going. When a woman uses seduction to entrap a man into a relationship or marriage, she cannot expect him to have the vision to lead in the relationship. That is what this spirit does: It takes away men's courage and authority to lead!

Judges 16:21

Then the Philistines took him and put out his eyes and brought him down to Gaza. They bound him with bronze fetters, and he became a grinder in the prison.

In my more than twenty years of ministry, I have met and counseled many women. Although I have not met many Jezebels, most of the women have been attacked and influenced by the Jezebel spirit. I myself have not been spared. My personal attack from the Jezebel spirit was obvious the moment I stepped onto American soil, and it heightened as Derek and I started the church and began to disciple people. God loves America, but Satan hates what America stands for and seeks to destroy the nation's spiritual heritage. Residing in California, I can see the powers of darkness fiercely trying to destroy relationships between people, marriages, and leaders (especially leaders of the church). Although many claim to attend church, few are truly planted and committed to discipleship. A high level of mistrust exists between people because of broken-down relationships. Most people resist committing to their local church and begin church-hopping. The Church in this territory has become powerless to influence society and, to say the least, have the power to confront the principalities that are coming against Her.

On his website, Donald J. Ibbitson, president of Above & Beyond Counseling Ministries, notes twelve warning signs that the Jezebel spirit is influencing someone. They were extracted from the book *Jezebel's Puppets* by Jennifer LeClaire; I think it is good to share them with you. While we might see some of these warning signs in people we know, we should examine ourselves to see if we also are entertaining similar intentions or exhibiting similar behaviors. To shut the door to their effects on society, we must first shut the door to their effects in the church. The church is made up of people, hence God's people, who (and especially women) need to learn to watch out for these signs. They must come before God to repent and address the root issues that have allowed these influences and their effects.

Twelve Indicators of a Jezebel Spirit at Work

(1) People influenced by a spirit of Jezebel have fear issues of rejection. They control others so that they will not be hurt. Generally, there is a history of trauma or abuse.

(2) They target the headship. They offer free help to be their top assistant because they want their protection. It hides from the leader's view but manifests in front of others.

(3) They make commitments and promises quickly and use recommendations from others to impress others.

(4) They seem super-spiritual in an exaggerated way to gain acceptance and attention. They have their own agenda. They are looking for disciples of their own. They whine until they get their way.

(5) They isolate and pit people against each other privately and individually behind closed doors.

(6) They play the victim. They are never wrong. They blame everyone else. They play on compassion to block discernment.

(7) They use false humility and feel entitled or owed something.

(8) They are not accountable to anyone and often accuse others of being a Jezebel.

(9) They look for others who are hurt and wounded to mentor them.

(10) They accuse people falsely.

(11) They operate with insecurity.

(12) They initiate witchcraft prayers based on selfish motivation.

Does any of this sound or look familiar? If you are under a leadership authority where Jezebel is at work, you may well be a target for torment. How can you tell? LeClaire went on to offer six indicators to consider:

Six Signs That Jezebel Is Directing Attacks Against You

(1) You become fearful.

(2) You isolate yourself more.

(3) You experience unreasonable exhaustion.

(4) Your thoughts and dreams become sexually perverse.

(5) Strange and prolonged illnesses hinder you.

(6) Freak accidents become commonplace.[1]

Revelation 2:20 warns that we must not tolerate this spirit from operating in our sphere of influence. The Jezebel spirit, when left unopposed, will destroy ministries, churches, marriages, and businesses. If God is putting His finger in areas of your life that you have allowed

---

[1] https://aandbcounseling.com/12-warning-signs-person-influence-jezebel-spirit

this spirit to operate in, then you must repent immediately and renounce your agreement with it. Do not brush this aside and belittle its effect. Most people are the spirit's victims without realizing it; but now that your eyes are open, you need to be vigilant in keeping this spirit out of your life. Full-blown Jezebels are aware yet willfully give themselves to be influenced by it. However, this is not a spirit to fight alone. Seek out church leadership whom you trust, and open your heart to be counseled, healed, and delivered. If your church is not equipped to handle this, Christian counseling and deliverance may be necessary to help determine your next step.

Satan sets principalities, such as the Jezebel spirit, to manipulate women through their unhealed hearts to cause destruction, mainly in the area of relationships.

Revelation 12:15

So, the serpent spewed water out of his mouth like a flood after the woman, that he might cause her to be carried away by the flood.

John wrote that Satan has a personal vendetta against the woman who represents the church. Satan sets principalities, such as the Jezebel spirit, to manipulate women through their unhealed hearts to cause destruction, mainly in the area of relationships. The Jezebel spirit does not work alone; it has a close cousin, and along with this ally spirit, it wreaks havoc in the church and cripples the power of the church to bring order to society. I am referring to the spirit of Leviathan.

Operation of the Leviathan Spirit

Leviathan is a metaphorical reference in Scripture that draws from the image of a great serpentine sea creature. It describes a spirit that works to twist words and perceptions to disrupt and destroy relationships between the people of God.

Isaiah 27:1

In that day the Lord with His severe sword, great and strong,
Will punish Leviathan the fleeing serpent,
Leviathan that twisted serpent;
And He will slay the reptile that is in the sea.

Isaiah referred to a spirit and employed a metaphor to describe it. In Scripture, this spirit is regarded as a sea monster or seen as a serpent of some type. The very word "Leviathan" means "to twist." The Leviathan spirit has many characteristics, but it mainly manifests itself as pride.

It preys upon very real hurts and wrongs. However, through stirring up pride within you, it blocks you from truly acknowledging what was done and sincerely asking God to "heal me!" Leviathan is a prideful spirit that won't allow you to honestly confront your own faults and dysfunctions. This spirit causes you to be deceived and embrace opinions and see them as revelation truth, calling what is right wrong and vice versa!

Leviathan is a twisting serpent that wraps itself around you and covers you so that you cannot see, hear, or speak properly. It blinds you from seeing what God is doing in the reconstruction work of your life; he covers your ears so you can't hear what God is trying to tell your heart, and he'll try to silence you, so even though you maintain the ability to talk, nothing that you say makes sense or aligns with what God is trying to do. Your words, if he is successful, will become devoid of any power. Ultimately, Leviathan attempts to squeeze the life out of you until it's all gone.

No other person in the Bible understood the deadly power of this spirit more than Job. He had a firsthand battle with this demon and after winning it, Job received a double portion of the wealth he lost and gained seven sons and three daughters. Oftentimes, the book of Job leaves readers disturbed that God would allow a righteous man to experience the things Job did. In our attempt to understand God's goodness through our limited human minds, we often equate what we feel and think is good to what God would define as good. According to Scripture, Satan sought God's permission to take Job's wealth, health, and family, bringing Job into desperate pain. Job's friends' attempt to comfort him backfired and created a rift. In his pain, Job had become self-righteous and irreconcilable.

God wisely unmasked a trait that keeps people from being healed and restored after loss. In our pain, we can become self-righteous—"I didn't do anything to deserve this, God! Your people did me wrong! You did me wrong!" This pride creates a wedge in our relationship with God and His people, just as it did with Job. He defended himself in pride, denying any sin in his life. He could not see the hands and heart of God in the people that were sent to comfort him. He even demanded a hearing from God! God began to rebuke him, *"Where were you when I laid out the foundations of the earth?"* (Job 38:4) and put him in his place, saying, *"Would you condemn me so that you can be justified"* (Job 40:8)? Through this painful episode, God showed Job what had subtly crept into his life that otherwise would not have been detected if not for what had happened.

> **Leviathan will whisper in your mind and disguise himself as your own voice until you come into full agreement with him.**

In God's closing argument with Job in chapter 41, He outlines Leviathan's frightening arrogance and destructive nature. Referring to this creature, He says his *"scales are his pride"* (v.15), adding that his heart is *"as hard as stone"* (v.24). Finally, God concludes by saying he is *"the king over all the children of pride"* (v.34). Job, in his sorrow, rose up in pride rather than clothed himself with humility. He allowed pride and pain to rule him and in turn twisted his perception. Like Leviathan, he became twisted, hardened, and irreconcilable. When pride hardens your heart, your mind gives in to wrong perceptions of God, people, and your situations. Finally, we release hell's fire through our words!

Job 41:18-21

His sneezing's flash forth light and his eyes are like the eyelids of the morning.
Out of his mouth go burning lights; sparks of fire shoot out.
Smoke goes out of his nostrils, as from a boiling pot and burning rushes.
His breath kindles coals, and a flame goes out of his mouth.

This spirit's danger is in its tongue, and he wants to use it to poison yours. Every so often, Leviathan will whisper in your mind and disguise himself as your own voice until you come into full agreement with him (v.3). When the covenant is made, you will be used as a weapon to imbue its effects of pride, manipulation, conspiracy, and mistrust (v.4-6). His objective is to poison your tongue so that you will bring destruction through your confessions! Look at how James describes our tongue.

James 3:5-8

Even so the tongue is a little member and boasts great things. See how great a forest a little fire kindles! And the tongue is a fire, a world of iniquity. The tongue is so set among our members that it defiles the whole body and sets on fire the course of nature; and it is set on fire by hell. For every kind of beast and bird, of reptile and creature of the sea, is tamed and has been tamed by mankind. But no man can tame the tongue. It is an unruly evil, full of deadly poison.

Eve The Last

The Bible warns us that no man can tame the tongue! Similarly, Job 41:9-10 says no hope exists to overcome Leviathan; we shall be overwhelmed if we ever dare stir him up. Leviathan's end goal is to destroy relationships, especially covenant ones! When pain and loss pierce us, wounds can settle in our souls. The enemy plays off of these wounds and creates separations in our families, churches, and networks. He twists words, distorts intentions, and prompts us to react out of pain instead of love. A train wreck always results from this.

Effects of the Leviathan Spirit

(1) Cold Love toward One Another

The influence of the Leviathan spirit sets fires that devour love and covenant, ultimately robbing God's people of hope and weakening their influence in the world. One primary means of sowing this destruction is to distort perceptions of what has been said, causing those under its influence to hear innocent things in a twisted way. People then pass their twisted perceptions to one another, now cloaked as truth, thus injecting poison into relationships and weakening bonds of love and unity.

Matthew 24:10-12

And then many will be offended, will betray one another, and will hate one another. Then many false prophets will rise up and deceive many. And because lawlessness will abound, the love of many will grow cold.

(2) Mistrust toward Leadership

Oftentimes, it will masquerade as the Holy Spirit and under the guise of "discernment," subtly questioning the motivations and character of leadership. We then see people in authority through tainted lenses, making us filter their words and actions as other than they really were, often the very opposite of what was intended. Under Leviathan's influence, statements and actions can be taken out of their context to make them into something they were not.

When distorting truth and reality doesn't work, this demonic spirit will turn to tormenting lies, but these lies will be crafted in such a way as to appear to be the truth, creating a wave of conspiracy. Basic trust is the foundation of all relationships. When that trust is in question, the oneness of the body of Christ fractures.

(3) Misplaced Blame toward God

The kingdom of God thrives on honor—honor for God and for one another. It expands when we focus on what God is doing in people and in the church, rather than on what we judge Him not to be doing.

Once we begin to focus on what we feel He is not doing, we open the door to the Leviathan spirit to cause us to blame, torment, and criticize our leaders or authority. We then begin to measure the leadership God has put in place and find it broken and wanting in some way. This leads us to fall into the trap of seeing only the flaws in one another rather than the glory God is creating and the changes He is making in those with whom we've been called to walk. This will eventually make us blame God for not intervening in our situations.

The Leviathan spirit has one agenda: to break unity and covenant relationships to isolate us so that we cannot function (individually and corporately) as the gateway of heaven's influence. Honor transports anointing and authority throughout the body of Christ so as to help her fulfill her destiny. Our relationships with one another are crucial to growing us and helping us fulfill our purpose. Paul describes the joints in the body of Christ as keys to our supply (Eph. 4:16). Dislocated spiritual joints are painful and disabling to our unity and growth as the church—a real coup for the enemy.

Starving Leviathan

So, we must not allow the Leviathan spirit to have a place in our soul. Pride is the problem. When we justify ourselves, pride hardens our hearts and deceives us (1 John 1:8). We then open ourselves up to deception, and that's when the twisting begins. Division and separation start to take place in our relationships. We begin to second-guess intentions and others' words—*"What did he mean by that?"* With the right amount of demonic spin, confusion and suspicion are sown between even the best of friends. The enemy twists things just a little bit more each time, and if we don't discern it, things can snap. Even pastors and spiritual leaders can fall into a spirit of division and part ways over unimportant matters (see Acts 15:36-40). The trick is always the same: twisting and separation, twisting and separation—and snap!

The problem is pride; the solution is humility. When we let the Lord reveal our pride, we can turn and be free. James 4:10 instructs us *"to humble ourselves in the sight of the Lord, for He will lift us up."* When we lower our fleshly desire to rebut, retort, and get justice, God will lift up our spirits to see the "exit" sign to get out of pride's entrapment. When we step into the light, Leviathan cannot touch us and feed on our carnality. If we refuse pride, but clothe ourselves with humility, we will starve out the spirit of Leviathan from our lives.

Word-twisting is central to Leviathan's operation. The serpent defeated Eve by twisting God's words. *"Did God really mean that? You won't die if you eat of the tree ..."* (see Gen. 3:4-5). Adam and Eve were quickly divided from God and each other, and a devastating fallout resulted. The Bible says that in response to that, God raised up a Second Adam and

"He has put all things under His feet" (1 Cor. 15:27). In like manner, God is training a generation of a Second Eve who shall not be deceived but will know how to defeat the lying serpent! Joined as one with the Second Adam, she will confront the principalities and powers, restore the people, and establish the kingdom!

Operation of the Absalom Spirit

Although the Bible is not explicit in naming this spirit, the term "Absalom spirit" is commonly accepted in the Charismatic faith and deliverance ministries; it refers to the demonic influence that comes through a person to divide a people and usurp the authority of an appointed leader. An Absalom spirit is named after Absalom, the third son of David, who built an open rebellion against his father. This is how Absalom stole the hearts of the people and began his coup:

> **"Absalom spirit" comes through a person to divide a people and usurp the authority of an appointed leader.**

2 Sam. 15:1-6

After this it happened that Absalom provided himself with chariots and horses, and fifty men to run before him. Now Absalom would rise early and stand beside the way to the gate. So it was, whenever anyone who had a lawsuit came to the king for a decision, that Absalom would call to him and say, "What city are you from?" And he would say, "Your servant is from such and such a tribe of Israel." Then Absalom would say to him, "Look, your case is good and right; but there is no deputy of the king to hear you." Moreover Absalom would say, "Oh, that I were made judge in the land, and everyone who has any suit or cause would come to me; then I would give him justice." And so it was, whenever anyone came near to bow down to him, that he would put out his hand and take him and kiss him. In this manner Absalom acted toward all Israel who came to the king for judgment. So, Absalom stole the hearts of the men of Israel.

Absalom would sit near the city gate and intercept those who came to the king to settle a matter. He particularly looked for discontented or troubled people and would sympathize with them. He would sow the idea that if he were the leader, they would get the justice that they so deserved. Through time, he stole the hearts of the people away from the one God put in authority and transferred that affection to himself. Before David could do anything, this spirit seduced his top guys and they defected!

The Absalom spirit gains access to people who are experiencing prolonged frustrations with their lives, marriages, or ministries, or just generally with where they are in life. However, instead of turning to God, they try to build their sense of worth through what they do. Nonetheless, whatever they pursue usually leads them back to the same place of frustration, discouragement, and anger, much like what Solomon described in Ecclesiastes 5:17.

Ecclesiastes 5:17 (NLT)

Throughout their lives, they live under a cloud—frustrated, discouraged, and angry.

When an Absalom spirit is at work in a church or business, you will notice turmoil and confusion. People will usually pick on a weakness in the system and through complaints and gossip stir up the emotions of others to come into agreement with them. Their complaints may be factual, yet their intentions are never to solve the problem but to highlight the incompetence of the person in authority. For example, the Bible says that we are to treat all with honor and hold the elderly in esteem as we would our own parents. Some people may not feel that this is practiced well in the church. The person influenced by the Absalom spirit would then take on the offense and rally supporters to accuse the leadership rather than approach them to discuss how the church can do better. The Absalom spirit attempts to satisfy legitimate needs using manipulation, and he believes he can do the job better than the one on top. John Burton, author of *Covens in the Church,* listed several indicators of an Absalom spirit and provided eight signs that you may be under the influence of Absalom.

Some Indicators of an Absalom Spirit

(1) They have big dreams but blame others for blocking those dreams.

(2) They feel their perceived level of wisdom is being ignored or their super gifts are not being put to use.

(3) They have false criteria; Absalom judged everything by his own criteria.

(4) A modern Absalom gets offended at leadership, then secretly arranges the subtle "execution" of the leader's reputation, achievements, or integrity.

(5) An Absalom spirit typically harbors camouflaged bitterness, unresolved offenses, disappointments, and anger.

(6) An Absalom spirit thrives on hidden agendas, concealed strategies, and secret alliances.

(7) Absalom is a master of manipulation and flattery.

(8) Absalom feeds his followers with his fault-finding and critical spirit.

(9)   An Absalom spirit exhibits false humility, yet proudly believes he is wiser and better than the appointed leader (2 Sam. 15:5).

Eight Signs That You May Be under Absalom's Influence

(1)   Gossip: This should be the easiest indicator, yet even the most seasoned Christians fall victim to the spirit of gossip. I've discovered that very few really understand what gossip really is. Here's my favorite definition: Gossip is any discussion about a person or an entity (such as a church, group, or business) that the person or leader of the entity would disapprove of. Would your pastor approve of your discussion about the church? If not, you are under Absalom's influence.

(2)   Right versus Wrong: Are you living in the tree of the knowledge of good and evil by attempting to prove yourself right and your leaders wrong? Or, are you living in the Tree of Life that results in honoring and serving them?

(3)   Contrary Visions: You and others in the church may see the need for something, such as a soup kitchen, small group ministry, or an evangelism emphasis. While this may be a valid need, you have to ask, "Does it agree with the specific vision of my church?" All churches aren't assigned to have soup kitchens, for example. It's important to come under the vision of the house and leave other focuses on your shelf until God enables you to run with them.

(4)   Gathering Others: Are you seeking support for your viewpoint? If you are gathering other people around you who share your concerns, you can know that the same thing happened in the story of Absalom.

(5)   Stealing Hearts: As you gather others, are you stealing their hearts, or are you affirming the pastor or leader they have been assigned to by God? Absalom stole the hearts of people who were under the care of David by listening to their complaints. Always call people to be loyal to their leaders and to approach them, not you, with their complaints.

(6)   Disengaging: Are you running strong with the leader, or are you shrinking back into a smaller group of disgruntled people?

(7)   Matthew 18: Are you applying Matthew 18 protocol to situations you are concerned about? Do you approach leadership alone with your concerns, or do you violate Matthew 18 by involving other people and seeking their counsel?

(8)   Division: Have you considered aborting your assignment in the church God planted you in by dividing off into another church? A lot of churches are born out of rebellion in the spirit of Absalom. Is this a desire of your heart? Or, are you willing to grow through the challenge in your current church?

Though the signs just discussed are written primarily in the context of the church, they are also applicable to the workplace or any context where people need to work together and submit to one another. The Absalom spirit is conniving, and it seeks to break the chain of command so that the corporate vision of the organization cannot be accomplished. The casualties are usually the people who have naively been used as political pawns in this power coup and the man or woman in leadership whose character has been assassinated. People influenced by Absalom rarely can trust anyone. Often plagued by a sense that they know better than their leaders, they find it hard to submit and work together. Oftentimes, they move from job to job and church to church.

E The Last ve

Just like Jezebel, we must not tolerate the Absalom spirit nor let a person afflicted with it to remain in power and in their place of influence. We must attempt to expose the works of these spirits, with the hope to bring the person under its influence back to their senses. This requires the work of the Holy Spirit and much wisdom. However, if all else fails, to protect the greater good, our last resort would be to part ways. If you are dealing with a spouse who exhibits the Absalom spirit, go on the offense in your intercession and allow the Holy Spirit to work through your prayers to bring revelation to him. Seek counsel from the intercession or deliverance ministry in your church, and partner with them to see complete deliverance.

Finally, are you exhibiting some of these traits? If you feel that the Holy Spirit is convicting you, come as you are to the presence of God and allow Him to shine understanding about the entry point for this spirit. Did disappointment open the door, or did an offense with an authority figure cause you to respond to this influence? This spirit is deadly and seeks to destroy you and through you destroy your company, care group, or church. Come before God today, and let Him have His way in your heart. Let Him bring you back to the place of innocence so that you can fulfill your God-given destiny. When a woman's heart is not healed, she is vulnerable to the influence of evil more than the influence of God.

Today, God is raising up the New Eve and training her to live free from these demonic influences, have the authority to push them back, free her people from destruction, and bring her people into His abundant life! In the next chapter, we will look at why God allows us to go through brokenness and how that journey is instrumental for our empowerment.

Chapter 8

The Power of a Broken Heart

G od created Eve to live in innocence and freedom. Ordained to be a helper to the man, He designed her with many hidden abilities and powers. Such powers that come from within required her to uncover them through time. The devil, knowing her calling and sensing her vulnerability, redirected her and restricted what she could do. He tempted her to transgress against the instruction of Adam, which came from God, causing her to break her covenant with God and man. Adam's rejection of her began the breaking of her heart.

"Pastor Susan, why did God allow me to go through this pain if He loves me?" Women I minister to have asked me this question many times. Incomprehensible as it may be, there is power in a broken heart when it's totally surrendered to God. God loved King David very much. Although David was broken and flawed, God saw who he was at his core; He saw in David a heart that He could mold into a masterpiece. Likewise, God wants to mold us into His masterpiece. Through you, He wants to paint a beautiful picture of your life, marriage, family, and future. Will you

let him? Will you allow him to mold and shape you into the person He wants you to be?

Jeremiah 29:11 (MSG)

I know what I'm doing. I have it all planned out—plans to take care of you, not abandon you, plans to give you the future you hope for.

God has it all planned out! God allowed Adam to break Eve's heart so that He could restore it and make it stronger. It was the devil's plan to restrict Eve, but God's intention was to set her free, through the breaking! In the wise words of singer Miranda Lambert: *"Happiness ain't prison, but there's freedom in a broken heart!"*

Live Openly and Expansively!

Ernest Shurtleff Holmes was an American New Thought writer, teacher, and leader who wrote, *"Life is not just something to be endured. It is to be lived in joy, in fullness without limit."*

Our Creator desires for us to live in fullness and without limit. He declares in Isaiah 54:2-3 that we should "enlarge," "stretch out," "lengthen our cords," and "strengthen our stakes," and emphasizes again that we shall expand to the right and to the left. Second Corinthians 6, in The Message translation, says it so beautifully.

2 Corinthians 6:11-13 (MSG)

Dear, dear Corinthians, I can't tell you how much I long for you to enter this wide-open, spacious life. We didn't fence you in. The smallness you feel comes from within you. Your lives aren't small, but you're living them in a small way. I'm speaking as plainly as I can and with great affection. Open up your lives. Live openly and expansively!

This command to expand our lives echoes the instruction to Adam in creation: *"Be fruitful and multiply; fill the earth and subdue it; have dominion over the fish of the sea, over the birds of the air, and over every living thing that moves on the earth."* This command was given "to them"; both man and woman are called to be the extension of God's dominion on Earth. God chose to work through men to permeate His goodness and expand His kingdom. In Matthew 13, Jesus likened the kingdom to a grain of mustard seed that a man took and sowed in his field. Though it started small, in the end it will grow into a huge tree, larger than all the garden plants so that *"the birds of the air can come and make nests in its branches."* He also uses how leaven works through flour to illustrate that no matter how small and inconspicuous the kingdom, it shall grow until it's fully visible. In fact, the kingdoms of the world will become *"the kingdoms of our Lord and of His Christ, and He shall reign forever and ever"* (Rev. 11:15)! Yet, where does the kingdom of God first exist? It exists first in your heart!

Luke 17:20-21

Now when He was asked by the Pharisees when the kingdom of God would come, He answered them and said, "The kingdom of God does not come with observation; nor will they say, 'See here!' or 'See there!' For indeed, the kingdom of God is within you."

The call to live a life of dominion is not for our luxury but to fully manifest the kingdom and its glory. Hence, to fulfill that call we need to understand that we need to look within; we need to look at our hearts. In fact, how we live depends on the condition of our hearts!

Proverbs 4:23 (CSB)

Guard your heart above all else, for it is the source of life.

Eve The Last

A woman's heart is the wellspring of life and the secret place upon which God can change the world!

Chapter 6 spoke about the heart being our power source and that it has to be fully aligned with God, our True North. The heart of a woman carries enough power, like that of a military submarine, to destroy the enemy's camp. It is strong enough to love the unlovable and gather the rebels and transform them into sons. It contains the sensitivity that connects her to the Holy Spirit and empowers her to hear, see, and speak prophetically. A woman's heart is the wellspring of life and the secret place upon which God can change the world! Having said that, a heart hardened by the hardness of this world will be void of all the powers just mentioned, and though she is gifted and harbors high aspirations, she will not achieve what God desires to see.

Jeremiah 4:3

For thus says the Lord to the men of Judah and Jerusalem:
"Break up your fallow ground,
And do not sow among thorns."

Just like a farmer planting seeds for a harvest, we need to break open the fallow grounds so that the ground can embrace the seed and take root. If you plant a seed too shallow, it won't have enough soil cover to support the germinating top growth. The rule of thumb: Plant a seed three times the depth of the size of the seed. If your seeds are very tiny, just the barest covering of soil will be enough. For larger seeds, the depth varies with the size of the seed. Luke 8 illustrates the Word of God as a seed. Hence, if we want the Word to transform us, we must allow the seed to go deeper. The deeper the seed, the bigger the tree. This has nothing to do with the size of the seed in the context of the Word. It has everything to do with how deep the Word is kept in the heart. In the same passage, Jesus told His followers the parable of the sower who went out to sow his seed. Depending on the condition of the ground the seed fell upon, the seed was either devoured by birds, withered, or choked up by thorns. But the seeds that fell on good ground sprang up and *"yielded a crop a hundredfold"* (Luke 8:8)! The ground represents our hearts. To see such transformation in and through our lives, the Lord needs to break up our hardened hearts!

The Purpose of Suffering

Hosea 10:12

Sow for yourselves righteousness;
Reap in mercy;
Break up your fallow ground,
For it is time to seek the Lord,
Till He comes and rains righteousness on you.

To break our hearts, God allows us to go through sufferings. Suffering is painful and perplexing, yet it has its purpose. In our world, suffering is a reality, one caused by sin and a reality that breaks the heart of God. Instead of shielding us from this world, God uses the things that we suffer to bring the hidden things of the woman to a place of visibility. In an earlier chapter, we mentioned the law of process. The Lord Jesus had to go through this same process in order for salvation to come to all men—the fulfillment of His assignment. For the believer, suffering is not only for eternity's sake but also for purification in this life. Through the things that we suffer, God molds, sharpens, and strengthens us. Suffering can be brought about because of God's discipline (Heb. 12:6). It can also be for a cutting back so that greater fruitfulness can be found in our lives

(John 15:2). Suffering can even be an effort to prevent us from pride and independence (Prov. 16:5). No matter the reason for the suffering, God uses trials and tribulations to mold us into the image of His perfect Son, sharpen our focus, develop our character, and strengthen our faith in Him and His promises (James 1:2–4; 1 Pet. 1:6–7).

Suffering is not in itself virtuous, nor is it a sign of holiness. God uses suffering to get our attention to make us confront our hearts' conditions. Through suffering, He wants us to draw near to Him and seek His perspective. By doing so, we can grow in the stature of Christ and accomplish His purposes. We are not to pursue suffering, but when it comes, with the right response from us, it will have eternal and empowering effects. Jesus suffered not because of His own wrongdoings but because of His Father's will.

> **A broken heart that can embrace the pain of life, allowing God to restore it, is a catalyst for great courage to live without limits!**

Hebrews 5:8-9

Though He was a Son, yet He learned obedience by the things which He suffered. And having been perfected, He became the author of eternal salvation to all who obey Him.

Our Lord performed many signs and taught much wisdom while He was on Earth, but people were attracted to Him for His vulnerability. He showed great compassion for the people who followed Him. He healed, delivered, and taught them out of His compassionate love for them. He wept for them when He saw they had no one to lead them. *"Jesus wept"* (John 11:35) centers on the fact that Jesus cried. Why was He crying knowing that Lazarus would rise again? He wasn't crying because Lazarus was dead. At that moment, the sorrow of the people who mourned without hope moved Jesus to tears! This is the power of a broken-open heart! It has the vulnerability to feel others' pain yet contains the courage upon which the same others can hold on for a better tomorrow. A broken heart that can embrace the pain of life, allowing God to restore it, is a catalyst for great courage to live without limits!

Rumi, the well-known thirteenth-century Muslim Persian poet, has a famous saying:

"We have to keep breaking the heart until it opens."

The well-respected pastor of Saddleback Church, Rick Warren, author of *The Purpose-Driven Life*, said this: *"In the case of Jesus, they didn't have to break his legs, because he had already died. But just to make sure, they stuck a spear in his side. Water and blood came out of the chest cavity, which, doctors say, only happens if the heart rips. You can call it what you want, but Jesus died of a broken heart!"*

Jesus died of a broken heart. He died in the flesh so that we can live in the spirit. He allowed His heart to be broken so that He can have the power to heal ours. The broken heart exposes us to the pain of life, but the healed heart holds the power to live a victorious life.

The Japanese Art of Kintsugi

While attending a church service in Singapore years back, the pastor spoke about the importance of embracing our brokenness. He illustrated his message through the art of Kintsugi, a centuries-old Japanese art of repairing broken pottery and transforming it into a new work of art with gold, the traditional metal used in Kintsugi. The name of the technique is derived from the words *"kin"* (golden) and *"tsugi"* (joinery), which translate to mean "golden repair." Instead of throwing away the broken pottery or hiding the cracks, the Kintsugi philosophy encourages just the opposite. It believes that if an object has been damaged, it has more of a history and should therefore be celebrated and highlighted rather than hidden or discarded.

Kintsugi centers on embracing the flawed or imperfect. Instead of covering up the imperfections, the art of Kintsugi embraces the scars and cracks. Through restoration, the art form turns the object into something beautiful to look at and valuable to keep. This is truly a contradiction of our social norm, especially in California where we are quick to hide our flaws and only reveal what is perfect or rather, what we think is perfect. Women are quick to address the imperfections of their outward appearance yet oftentimes do so little to focus on their inner spiritual conditions, especially the condition of their hearts.

When we allow God to penetrate deep into our hearts to the cracks, He infuses himself into our lives.

Kintsugi is a powerful metaphor for the human experience. In life, we can't avoid making mistakes or suffering damage. Rather than shield us from all bad things, God allows us to go through what we can bear so that we can grow wiser, become stronger, and increase in our value. When we allow God to penetrate deep into our hearts to the cracks, He infuses himself into our lives. As a transitional metal, gold symbolizes flexibility on our spiritual path while life experience galvanizes our faith. One of the more valued elements, gold represents great value. Because of its resistance to heat and acid, it symbolizes strength, eternity, and perfection. It is a picture of God and its divine nature. When you allow God to journey with you through your pain, and you yield your heart to be healed, you will see transformation first on the inside and then the outward manifestations.

In Kintsugi, every repaired piece is unique because of the randomness with which ceramic shatters and the irregular patterns formed that are enhanced with the use of metals. Likewise, all of us have been broken in different shapes and forms and by different people, yet we all can be healed by the same Maker; from that, others can see the handprint of God on our lives—the same Master but different masterpieces.

Be Diligent to Guard, Grow, and Govern Your Heart!

Breaking in life is inevitable, but healing and the depth of such healing depends upon the individual. Healing is not automatic and no, it is not a matter of time. A person may not exhibit the effects of trauma and may appear functional, but without a complete healing by the Healer, she is not fully living. Do you desire to live open and expansive lives? Do you want to keep growing and not be limited by people, circumstances, and your own apprehensions? Do you want to see God and partner with Him in this end-time dispensation? If you answer "yes," then you need to do three things with your heart.

(1) Guard Your Heart

Within your heart lies the treasure chest of your life, so we must guard our hearts with all diligence. Guarding your heart involves protecting it from wrong things, but it also involves inspecting what garbage may already be there. Your heart is like a garden, and you need to know what is growing in your garden. When I first moved to California, the state was experiencing a prolonged drought. "Brown" was the new "green" then. My yard was brown

We need to be aware of the trash in our hearts and remove it so that we can have a healthy garden of a heart.

all the time, and nothing we did helped the grass grow. However, about three years later, the rain came back and the drought ended. One morning, I woke up with the yard springing forth green! In my eagerness to keep it green, I instructed my gardener to make sure that he watered it sufficiently. Sheepishly, he answered, "Ma'am, sorry, but these are weeds, not grass." Feeling pretty embarrassed, I learned that if we do not know the difference between weeds and grass, we will let the weeds destroy our garden! As it is in our natural garden, so the same principle goes in the matters of our hearts. We need to be aware of the trash in our hearts and remove it so that we can have a healthy garden of a heart.

Some trash, such as moral corruption, perverse behavior, and evil acts, is easy to detect, and if we humble ourselves before God, He will give us the grace to repent and be restored. However, most of the trash, such as a lack of faith, unwillingness to forgive, materialism, pride, envy, jealousy, resentment, and false belief systems, will be covered up or easily ignored. We are all guilty of pushing the snooze button when it comes to these issues. We learned how to pretend they don't exist and use ministry and good works to compensate for how we feel on the inside. Ignoring the trash in our hearts can only last so long; at some point in time, the same trash will choke our hearts and cause a major heart blockage. Trash, big or small, is still trash.

Guarding your heart is the start, but growing it must be every woman's lifelong goal.

That is why God instructed the prophet Jeremiah to "root out," "pull down," "destroy," and "throw down." We cannot just root out or pull down this trash; working with God, we must utterly destroy and throw it down from having its place in our hearts. When we allow wounds to fester in our hearts and when we tolerate sin, we cannot come boldly before God and with authority ask for anything or pray for anyone. We certainly will not have the right assessment of our worth, and instead of being the extension of the works of the Holy Spirit, we will fight to be seen, heard, and acknowledged. A woman whose heart is filled with unhealed wounds cannot love others unreservedly, and any display of love is with the condition of her being loved the same way, if not more.

(2) Grow Your Heart

Guarding your heart is the start, but growing it must be every woman's lifelong goal. Christian growth is a lifetime cultivation of the heart—impulses and desires, conscious and unconscious. We need to focus on what is shaping our hearts. Growing the heart indicates a pursuit.

The Bible says that David was a man after God's own heart. David used all his energy toward pursuing God. He spent time with God. His inward life was more important than his outward activity. It was his highest priority, and he learned to work effectively from the inward to the outward. Out of our hearts flow our energy, insight, and influence for God. David let God penetrate his heart deeply. God was his one dominant passion.

Look at David. Though he was apparently a lover more than a fighter, he slayed the lion and the bear who came after his sheep. Though he was a young lad, he was not afraid of Goliath the giant. His heart for God caused him to be unafraid of his circumstances even when it appeared that he was at a disadvantage. Not only that, though he suffered much betrayal and injustice, he never stopped pursuing God. No matter how difficult, he often willed himself back to the place of his first love.

E^{The Last}ve

Psalm 27:1

The Lord is my light and my salvation;
Whom shall I fear?
The Lord is the strength of my life;
Of whom shall I be afraid?

David uttered these words because he knew God. Day after day while in the field meditating and worshiping Jehovah, God Himself taught David many things about His role as the Chief Shepherd. Through David caring for his sheep, God revealed to him how the One above was caring for him. As time developed, David became more and more enveloped in God's love. As David grew in His love for God, his heart grew. As his heart grew, he began to grow in his love for God's people and desire to defend God's name.

When Goliath, the giant, came to battle against the people of God, King Saul and all of Israel were dismayed and greatly afraid. But not so David because his love for God made him fearless and the enemy's attempt to humiliate God set a fiery indignation inside of him. In his eyes, none was greater than God and all must revere His name. David was so provoked that he spoke to the men who stood by him, saying, *"What shall be done for the man who kills this Philistine and takes away the reproach from Israel? For who is this uncircumcised Philistine, that he should defy the armies of the living God?"* God's love for David energized his heart, and his love for God empowered him to be a good shepherd over His people.

Upon Peter's restoration, the Lord asked him to not just love Him but to feed His lambs and tend to His sheep (John 21:15-17). To grow your heart, you must grow your love. A love that transforms in either direction cannot be done at arm's length. It requires courage to draw closer to someone and allow that someone to take a step closer into your inner world. That is frightening for a wounded heart but without which you cannot grow in your capacity to love. And without love, our ability to have faith is hindered. Love is the oil that fuels the engine of faith.

Galatians 5:6

For in Christ Jesus neither circumcision nor uncircumcision avails anything, but faith working through love.

A woman who knows that she has been forgiven much will love much. Like the sinful woman in Luke 7, set free by the forgiveness and love of Jesus, she rose up in courage and faith to enter the house of a Pharisee; in doing so, she went against all cultural norms of her time. Not deterred by the male spectators' scornful stares, she sought Jesus out to wash His feet with her tears, wipe them with her hair, kiss His feet, and anoint them with fragrant oil. A heart healed by God's love is freed of fear. First John 4:18 talks about the perfect (full-grown, mature) love casting out all fear. Just knowing that God loves us will not cast out fear because fear starts in the heart. So, the experience of such a love must start from the heart, and we must walk it out over and over again until it becomes full-grown and mature!

Do you want to encounter such a powerful love, one that propels you to have courage to attempt great things? Grow your love for your heavenly Husband by knowing Him intimately through His Word and through worship. Tell Him you want to know and love Him more. Cultivate your love for the things He loves most, which is His love for His body—the people that He calls His own. Just like David, would you love what He loves and hate what He hates? Would you pray, "Lord, let my heart beat as one with you. Let my heart break for what breaks yours and love as you love"?

(3) Govern Your Heart

When we begin to guard our hearts, we will see the things we must root out and destroy. The next step is to build and grow new things in our hearts. The Bible talks about growing the fruit of the Spirit, which is love, joy, peace, longsuffering, kindness, goodness, faithfulness, gentleness, and self-control. Against such, no law implies that a woman who has successfully developed these qualities in her life needs to be governed outwardly, for she is governed by what is on the inside. To govern implies to rule over by right of authority. As a believer, that authority must be the Word of God. David says it so aptly in Psalm 119.

Psalm 119:9-11

How can a young man cleanse his way?
By taking heed according to Your word.
With my whole heart I have sought You;
Oh, let me not wander from Your commandments!
Your word I have hidden in my heart,
That I might not sin against You.

Knowing where our power source lies to change our lives and that of others, we must be diligent to govern it. David teaches us to let God's instructions be imprinted in our hearts so that they will continue to align with God's. Romans 6:12 reminds us to *"not let sin reign in your mortal body, that you should obey it in its lusts."* Desiring to live a fruitful life, we must be one with God, and that oneness starts in our hearts.

John 15:4-5

Abide in Me, and I in you. As the branch cannot bear fruit of itself, unless it abides in the vine, neither can you, unless you abide in Me. I am the vine, you are the branches. He who abides in Me, and I in him, bears much fruit;

for without Me you can do nothing. If anyone does not abide in Me, he is cast out as a branch and is withered; and they gather them and throw them into the fire, and they are burned.

When we fully embrace the Word of God and submit to God's instruction, we begin aligning our values with God's values. We now give preference to what God wants rather than what we want or what others expect of us. Out of that, we begin to develop the spiritual wisdom and discernment to make wise choices; this brings order in place of chaos and sees fruitfulness in the place that once was barren. Building a stronghold for our Lord Jesus in our inward lives, we develop an appetite for holiness and a distaste for corruption. We reclaim our innocence yet are not naive to the works of spiritual darkness. When we give our hearts fully to the Lord, we are ready to journey with God to the destiny that God has prepared for us.

Proverbs 23:26

My son, give me your heart,
And let your eyes observe my ways.

Building a stronghold for our Lord Jesus in our inward lives, we develop an appetite for holiness and a distaste for corruption. We reclaim our innocence yet are not naive to the works of spiritual darkness.

The Second Eve

Eve, in her transgression, broke the covenant with man and God. God, on the other hand, was always working to restore that covenant with her. In fact, God loves women so much that He hurts when they hurt, and He mourns for the healing of His daughter.

Jeremiah 8:21-22

For the hurt of the daughter of my people I am hurt.
I am mourning;
Astonishment has taken hold of me.
Is there no balm in Gilead,
Is there no physician there?
Why then is there no recovery
For the health of the daughter of my people?

Depression, constant worry, unhealthy fear, unfounded anger, indifference, and so much more—these symptoms plague a shutdown heart. However, when we learn to submit through our brokenness, God infuses His divine nature into our hearts' cracks. Man's heart and God's heart becoming one produces the likeness of Christ in us. Hence, the symptom of a healed heart in a woman is her gentle, quiet, and submissive spirit.

1 Peter 3:3-5

Do not let your adornment be merely outward—arranging the hair, wearing gold, or putting on fine apparel—rather let it be the hidden person of the heart, with the incorruptible beauty of a gentle and quiet spirit, which is very precious in the sight of God. For in this manner, in former times, the holy women who trusted in God also adorned themselves, being submissive to their own husbands ...

As we approach the end-times, God is paving the way for His women to assume their place beside the men to rule in righteousness and restore the glory of the church. Unlike the first Eve, the Second Eve will have the wisdom to know the difference between good and evil. She will not be insubordinate. She will stand with the men in her generation and put Satan under their feet! With the help of the Holy Spirit, she will fulfill her destiny!

Chapter 9

Partnership with the Holy Spirit

John 14:26

But the Helper, the Holy Spirit, whom the Father will send in My name, He will teach you all things, and bring to your remembrance all things that I said to you.

The Promise of the Father

Earlier, we mentioned that women are meant to be the extension of the Holy Spirit on Earth. Both Eve and the Holy Spirit are referred to, by the Lord, as "the helper." Just as God created women to be the helpers of the men in their generation, the Holy Spirit is given to every believer to help them fulfill their assignments. Jesus, knowing the time of departure was drawing near, assembled His disciples and commanded them not to depart from Jerusalem until they had received the Holy Spirit—referring to the Third Person of the Holy Trinity as the *"Promise of the Father"* (Acts 1:4).

Eve The Last

This promise speaks to an agreement between the Father and the Son in which the giving of the Holy Spirit to the believers is a reward, provided a condition is met. The condition, of course, is that Jesus would give His life for us all on the cross. This act of sacrificing His Son to give us eternal life is the apex of the Father's love for us. While this eternal life comprises the life in heaven, it is not restricted to that. It also involves the abundant life that Jesus wants us to live while here on Earth (John 10:10). What kind of life is the abundant life? It is a blessed life, a life evidenced by God's favor. However, an abundant life is more than blessings; it also encompasses a life full of God's anointing and power. This abundant life is found in none other than the Spirit of God. Jesus was full of the Spirit of God, evident by the anointing that flowed from His life.

Luke 4:18-19

The Spirit of the Lord is upon Me,
Because He has anointed Me
To preach the gospel to the poor;
He has sent Me to heal the brokenhearted,
To proclaim liberty to the captives
And recovery of sight to the blind,
To set at liberty those who are oppressed;
To proclaim the acceptable year of the Lord.

Jesus lived that abundant life through the Holy Spirit. He was always connected to His Father through the Spirit and with His yieldingness, the anointing was made available for Him to perform His calling as the Messiah. The Bible tells us that this anointing came from the Holy Spirit, who taught Him concerning all things.

1 John 2:27

But the anointing which you have received from Him abides in you, and you do not need that anyone teach you; but as the same anointing teaches you concerning all things, and is true, and is not a lie, and just as it has taught you, you will abide in Him.

The Holy Spirit revealed to Jesus, through time, who He was: the Messiah in the Scripture. Revealing Him to be the Son of God, the Spirit further enlightened Jesus about His assignment and equipped Him to fully embrace His calling. In fact, the Bible refers to the Holy Spirit as the Spirit of adoption for the believers. The Spirit in our lives will give us a revelation of our birthright so that we can fully embrace our sonship (daughtership). He helps us build that intimacy with our Father so that we can call Him, "Dad!"

The Preeminence of the Holy Spirit

Jesus so wanted to give His followers this power that He urged them not to leave until they received the Holy Spirit. We know the result—they were filled with holy fire, which was evidenced by their ability to speak in another tongue!

Acts 1:8

But you shall receive power when the Holy Spirit has come upon you; and you shall be witnesses to Me in Jerusalem, and in all Judea and Samaria, and to the end of the earth.

The word "power" in the original Greek is ***"dunamis,"*** which means "dynamo," "dynamic," and "dynamite," implying that this abundant life is to be a source of forceful and explosive impact. And this power enables us to do more than what we can ask or think!

Eve The Last

Ephesians 3:20

Now to him who is able to do far more abundantly than all that we ask or think, according to the power at work within us.

The preeminence of the Holy Spirit is evident right from the beginning. He is the Spirit of creation, bringing into existence all things at the Word of the Father. From the onset of the creation of light in Genesis 1:3 to the virgin birth of the Lord Jesus Christ in the New Testament (Matt. 1:20), the Holy Spirit was involved in manifesting into reality what was declared through the Word of God (John 1:14). The book of Philippians refers to Him as the power that raised Christ from the dead.

Philippians 3:10

... that I may know Him and the power of His resurrection, and the fellowship of His sufferings, being conformed to His death.

The Spirit birthed the Lord, and upon His death resurrected Him on the third day. In resurrecting Jesus from the grave, God reminds us of His absolute sovereignty over life and death. The resurrection of Jesus Christ validates who Jesus claimed to be, namely the Son of God and the Messiah. The preeminence of the Holy Spirit is also over the church of Christ. In fact, the church was birthed in the Spirit with its founding members speaking in tongues! The New Testament church started with its members speaking in tongues. Believers have continued receiving the gift of the Holy Spirit with the ability to pray in a Spirit language, and the church will finish with praying in tongues. Speaking in tongues was a practice established in the foundation of the church.

To receive the gift of the Holy Spirit is a commandment of Jesus Christ. When Jesus commissioned the disciples to wait in Jerusalem until they received the Father's promise, He did not say, "Do this if you feel led to do so, or if it fits in your doctrinal or denominational beliefs, or if you have the time, or are so inclined, or feel comfortable about it." No! Jesus commanded them to wait until they received the gift of the Holy Spirit. He was conveying the reality that the most important thing they should do was receive the Holy Spirit. Since Jesus put such importance on this need, that is enough of a reason for every Christian to keep seeking God until they receive their Spirit prayer languages, evidenced by speaking in tongues.

When religious leaders questioned Jesus about which Mosaic Law was the most important, He simplified the Ten Commandments and clearly spelled out two commandments during His lifetime. The first was to *"love the Lord your God with all your heart, with all your soul, and with all your mind,"* and the second is like it: *"You shall love your neighbor as yourself"* (Matt. 22:37, 39). Whether it is ten or two, fulfilling God's commandments is no easy task, and I believe it is an impossible task without supernatural help! Let's take a look at the first commandment to love God. What is the measuring yardstick for the love that God expects of His disciples?

Luke 14:25-27

Now great multitudes went with Him. And He turned and said to them, "If anyone comes to Me and does not hate his father and mother, wife and children, brothers and sisters, yes, and his own life also, he cannot be My disciple. And whoever does not bear his cross and come after Me cannot be My disciple."

This is a tall order to fulfill and truly a heavy cross to bear. What about the second commandment, to love your neighbor? Jesus revealed the "new commandment" in John 13:34-35 while speaking to His disciples on the night Judas betrayed Him. He had just washed the disciples' feet, including Judas's, before He sent him away to his task at hand. After

E**ve** The Last

Judas was gone, Jesus spoke to the remaining eleven and gave them a new commandment.

John 13:34-35

A new commandment I give to you, that you love one another; as I have loved you, that you also love one another. By this all will know that you are My disciples, if you have love for one another.

But they ain't seen nothing yet! They were going to witness Him dying for every one of them in the room, including His enemies! In giving the new commandment, Jesus gave the directive for His disciples: *love*. The disciples were a mismatched crew of unlikely world-changers— some friends, some relatives, some strangers. They were rough around the edges, sinful, and as selfish as anyone else. Jesus transformed them and taught them what it was like to love as the Father loves.

In the Sermon on the Mount, Jesus taught about love in a way His disciples had never heard ...

Matthew 5:44-45

But I say to you, love your enemies, bless those who curse you, do good to those who hate you, and pray for those who spitefully use you and persecute you, that you may be sons of your Father in heaven ...

How can we love our enemies if we cannot find grace enough to forgive our loved ones for their transgressions? This brings to mind the incredible story of Pastor Richard Wurmbrand in the book *Tortured for Christ*. In Soviet Russia, he was severely persecuted for his belief in Jesus Christ. Imprisoned and tortured for fourteen years, he didn't give up his faith. Instead, he pledged his life to witness to the Russian soldiers and pray for those who tortured him.

Is this kind of love humanly possible? I am fully persuaded that such love expected by the Lord is not possible based on human effort. However, the Bible tells us that what is not possible with men is possible with God! I believe that is why the Lord would leave His disciples important instructions before He departed from this world. This most important instruction was, "You shall be filled with the power of the Holy Spirit!"

Acts 1:8

But you shall receive power when the Holy Spirit has come upon you; and you shall be witnesses to Me in Jerusalem, and in all Judea and Samaria, and to the end of the earth.

The disciples, obeying the Lord's instruction to stay in Jerusalem until such power was made available to them, stayed and prayed together in the Upper Room. What followed was a powerful picture of men and women praying in one accord without discrimination; the natural and spiritual family of Jesus praying in agreement for what they wanted to see, revival in their land! And the Spirit of revival came. The Holy Spirit engulfed the whole room and began to ignite the disciples. They started to exalt Jesus and proclaim Him in a tongue they had never learned!

The Holy Spirit came and bridged the great divide between men and women. He endorsed the women to be equally worthy to receive the power of God in the Person of the Holy Spirit. The outpouring of the Holy Spirit also addressed the racism between the Jews and the Gentiles of that time. The Holy Spirit instructed Peter, a Jew, to go to the house of Cornelius, the Gentile Centurion, to share the testimony of Jesus Christ. Let's read what Peter said …

Eve The Last

Acts 10:28

Then he said to them, "You know how unlawful it is for a Jewish man to keep company with or go to one of another nation. But God has shown me that I should not call any man common or unclean."

The prejudice between the Jews and Gentiles was dealt with the same day the Holy Spirit fell on Cornelius and his household in the midst of Peter's sermon. The Jews, who went with Peter, were astonished and could not deny that the gospel was not exclusive to them and that God truly loves the world and desires for none to perish. With that revelation, that day Peter and his team baptized Cornelius and his household in the name of the Lord! From that day onward, we read of the apostles who went around ensuring that those who believed received the baptism of the Holy Spirit.

Without a doubt, the Holy Spirit's outpouring is to equip the body of Christ to obey God's commandment to love God wholeheartedly and people fervently. Henceforth, after Jesus was resurrected and before He was called back to be with the Father, He instructed His disciples to wait until they were filled with the Holy Spirit.

When Christians meet ... their purpose is not—or should not be—to ascertain what is the mind of the majority, but what is the mind of the Holy Spirit—something which may be quite different.

— Margaret Thatcher, former British Prime Minister (1925-2013)

Jesus is the Lord over the church and in His absence, He has entrusted the Holy Spirit to be the custodian over her. However, instead of submitting to the Holy Spirit as her master, some, if not many, churches have rejected the Holy Spirit, treating Him as the mascot rather than the master. They have reduced the Holy Spirit to a standalone spiritual experience, or to being all about a denomination, or even about just speaking in another tongue. Many spirit-filled believers walk around with a form of godliness but void of power—the power to be a witness and to change their world.

2 Timothy 3:1-5

*But know this, that in the last days perilous times will come: For men will be lovers of themselves, lovers of money, boasters, proud, blasphemers, disobedient to parents, unthankful, unholy, unloving, unforgiving, slanderers, without self-control, brutal, despisers of good, traitors, headstrong, haughty, lovers of pleasure rather than lovers of God, **having a form of godliness but denying its power.***

When the church does not submit under the Lordship of His Spirit, the people within her walls become conceited and proud. With their self-serving attitudes, they hurt one another and as time passes the love of many will grow cold.

Matthew 24:8-14

*All these are the beginning of sorrows. Then they will deliver you up to tribulation and kill you, and you will be hated by all nations for My name's sake. And then many will be offended, will betray one another, and will hate one another. Then many false prophets will rise up and deceive many. **And because lawlessness will abound, the love of many will grow cold.** But he who endures to the end shall be saved. And this gospel of the kingdom will be preached in all the world as a witness to all the nations, and then the end will come.*

The Holy Spirit was sent for a purpose: to prepare the Bride to be worthy for the Groom.

The Holy Spirit was not sent to start a new denomination. He should not be restricted to just praying in tongues or performing signs and wonders; He was sent for a purpose: to prepare the Bride to be worthy for the Groom.

The Holy Spirit's Purpose

(1) Adoption and Identity

While salvation is made available to mankind through the death of Jesus on the cross, it can only be appropriated through the faith of the believer. Ephesians 2:8 reminds us that it is *"by grace you have been saved through faith, and that not of yourselves; it is the gift of God."* That faith was demonstrated through our confession. Romans 9:10 declares that *"with the heart one believes unto righteousness, and with the mouth confession is made unto salvation."*

When Jesus explained to Nicodemus that one must be born again to see the kingdom of God, He was referring to the work of the Holy Spirit that will bring about the adoption process. To God, salvation is not about having immortality as much as it is about having a Father and Son relationship with Him. Regeneration, which means being born again, is something the Spirit, not man, does. He is the One who brings us forth. He is the One who gives us new birth. He is the One who makes us the children of God. He is the Author of adoption.

Believers must yield to the Holy Spirit to be fully integrated into this new "family" that we have been adopted into. This, I must say, is not only a one-time experience, but a lifelong journey of understanding our Father's identity. How does He see me? What does He value? How would I "fit in" in this family? Failure to fully comprehend and be fully integrated (just like a natural child being adopted) will cause major identity issues. Identity formation happens throughout childhood and adolescence and continues to evolve and change throughout a person's life. Your identity is partly defined by where you feel like you "fit" within your family and with your peers. Likewise, our lack of understanding of how our Father feels about us and His plan for our lives would greatly sabotage this adoption process and cause us to hold on to our "old lives" out of fear of losing ourselves. The result? We cannot fully embrace our identity as sons and daughters and trust Him that He has the best interest at heart for each one of us individually. Without that trust, our lives will constantly be plagued with doubts and comparison as we try to find the evidence of the love that He has for us.

Our identity as the daughters of the most-high King is often the center of our crisis.

My daughters often love to play the "favorite daughter" game with me and their father. They try constantly to set us up to say who is our favorite, of which we often reply to them that we have no favorites and love them the same, just differently. In the same way, our Father loves us all the same. He does not play favorites, and He would not do anything to stir up jealousy or envy and put us against another. In fact, He openly declares that *"a sound heart is life to the body, but envy is rottenness to the bones"* (Prov. 14:30).

Our identity as the daughters of the most-high King is often the center of our crisis. Without a doubt, our true identity in God through Christ greatly impacts how we live and our choices. It is one thing to know in our heads and quite another to know it in our hearts. The Holy Spirit's main role is to imprint this identity (if we let Him) in our most inner being so that we can fully comprehend, with revelation, our heritage. Just as God declared to Jeremiah, *"Before I formed you in the womb*

I knew you; Before you were born I sanctified you; I ordained you a prophet to the nations" (Jer. 1:5), in the same way, we all came from the thought of God before we landed in our mothers' wombs. God knows us individually, and we are all fearfully and wonderfully made (Ps. 139:14). Embedded in our spirit is the image and likeness of God (Gen. 1:26).

The identity of Jesus being the first-born Son of God was also revealed to Him (Jesus) through a process in time. After His baptism, Jesus, empowered by the Holy Spirit, was led into the wilderness to be tempted by the devil. Three times, Satan tempted the Lord, and each time he would cast doubt on His identity, saying *"**IF** You are the Son of God …"* Satan wanted Jesus to prove that He was the Son of God, but the Lord never did, even though He could. By not receiving the evil one's instructions, He did not subject Himself to the powers of this world. Having fully identified Himself with His Father, He knew who He was, and He clearly knew His assignment. He did not need to defend Himself and definitely has no need to prove Himself to anyone else.

(2) Spiritual Maturity

As mothers, our role in our children's lives should not be limited to that of love and care. A mother knows that though her child depends on her in the early years, her main responsibility is to nurture the child to an emotional and mental maturity appropriate to her age. For a Christian mother, that responsibility extends into the area of her child's spirituality. Spiritual maturity, simply put, is to become like Jesus Christ. After salvation, every Christian begins spiritual growth with the intention to become spiritually mature. Spiritual maturity is the end goal of our Father for His children, and Ephesians 4 clearly communicates that.

Ephesians 4:13-14

Till we all come to the unity of the faith and of the knowledge of the Son of God, to a perfect man, to the measure of the stature of the fullness of Christ; that we should no longer be children, tossed to and from and carried about with every wind of doctrine, by the trickery of men, in the cunning craftiness of deceitful plotting …

According to Ephesians 4, our spiritual maturity is measured by how full we are of Christ. The evidence of that fullness is in the ability to know the truths of the kingdom and to walk in them. Therefore, a mature believer is not easily deceived, which is our Father's main concern. We see clearly the heart of a Father longing for His children not to be led astray. Even as the Lord reminded His disciples that ravenous wolves will come in sheepskin and deceive many in the body (Matt. 7:15), what happens when the sheep follow the shepherds not appointed by God? The prophet Jeremiah speaks of how the shepherds turned His people away on the mountain and brought them down to a hill that is plagued with much troubles. The sheep will find no rest, and eventually the predators will devour them (Jer. 50:6-7).

In John 10, Jesus establishes Himself as the True Shepherd and declares that His sheep shall hear His voice, and He knows them, and they follow Him only. How does one hear His voice? Where does this voice come from? It comes from within you (1 Kings 19:12). It is the same voice that whispered the will of the Father to Jesus. This is the voice of the Holy Spirit. Jesus, referring to the Holy Spirit as the Spirit of truth, states that He (the Holy Spirit) will not speak on His own authority. He will be that still small voice on the inside of you to help you hear the Shepherd's voice so that you will not blindly follow anyone who preaches the Word, but you will have the ability to discern the kind of fruits they bear (Matt. 7:16).

Therefore, the church must emphasize discipleship and spiritual growth. Spiritual infancy should not be casually accepted in the body. As we reach the world with the gospel and adopt them into the family, we need to commit to bringing them into spiritual maturity—to distinguish the voice of the Chief Shepherd in the people they follow. Like the Father, Jesus is concerned about the well-being of the flock and has specifically appointed us to shepherd others as well.

The Holy Spirit has a very important role: to speed up the maturity of God's people in the body.

Acts 20:28-30

Therefore take heed to yourselves and to all the flock, among which the Holy Spirit has made you overseers, to shepherd the church of God which He purchased with His own blood. For I know this, that after my departure savage wolves will come in among you, not sparing the flock. Also from among yourselves men will rise up, speaking perverse things, to draw away the disciples after themselves.

The Holy Spirit has a very important role: to speed up the maturity of God's people in the body. Romans 8:14 tells us that *"the sons of God are led by the Spirit and not their flesh nor their soul."* Without the Holy Spirit's help, people will be lost and confused, especially in the end-time. They will battle constantly with the lust of their flesh, the lust of their eyes, and the pride of life (1 John 2:16). The victory over these is found in the Spirit of God. When yielded to Him, we will find the liberty and grace to live as Christ and thus be free from the law. Without the Holy Spirit's guidance, men will find themselves torn between the desires of their flesh and obeying the Lord's Word.

Galatians 5:17-18

For the flesh lusts against the Spirit, and the Spirit against the flesh; and these are contrary to one another, so that you do not do the things that you wish. But if you are led by the Spirit, you are not under the law.

When we yield to the Holy Spirit, He gives us the grace to overcome the desires of our flesh that are in conflict with the will of God. When we will ourselves to follow His lead, we are free from the concerns about the law, as He who leads us is the fulfillment of such.

(3) Building Godly Relationships

Isaiah 11:1-2

There shall come forth a Rod from the stem of Jesse,
And a Branch shall grow out of his roots.
The Spirit of the Lord shall rest upon Him,
The Spirit of wisdom and understanding,
The Spirit of counsel and might,
The Spirit of knowledge and of the fear of the Lord.

The Holy Spirit's most crucial attribute would have to be the help He renders to us in building healthy, life-giving relationships.

The Bible describes the Holy Spirit as the Spirit of wisdom and understanding, counsel and might, and knowledge and the fear of the Lord. While these attributes are key factors for the success of a believer to navigate through this life, the most crucial attribute would have to be the help He renders to us in building healthy, life-giving relationships.

Let's start with the Spirit of knowledge and the fear of the Lord.

E_{ve}

Eve The Last

(A) The Spirit of Knowledge and the Fear of the Lord

God created us to feel fear, and fear instincts are an important drive to build self-control. Because we fear, we refrain from doing things we know can potentially hurt us or destroy us. Many of us let fear get in the way of doing something great or building life-changing relationships. But it's a mistake to think that the solution is to overcome fear in general. We can't and we shouldn't get rid of fear, totally. Instead, we should develop a healthy sense of fear in our lives because it will help us make wise decisions in our relationships. Where does a healthy sense of fear begin? The Bible tells us that we must first have the fear of the Lord!

Proverbs 1:7

The fear of the Lord is the beginning of knowledge,
But fools despise wisdom and instruction.

The "fear of the Lord" is a reverential awe of God; it is to honor and ascribe utmost value to God. It is recognizing the sacredness of the One we worship that moves a person to completely submit to His rulership and control, not because of fear of the consequences but out of love for God. The opposite of this is to treat as common what is sacred, which 1 Corinthians 11:26 warns us against.

1 Corinthians 11:26 (MSG)

You must never let familiarity breed contempt.

Don't be so overly familiar with God that you lose that sense of awe of God, forgetting that what lives on the inside of us is holy and sacred. When we lose the attitude of honoring God, we will lose the ability to honor the God in a person. So instead of honoring people for who they are in Christ, we honor them solely because of what they can do, what they have, or how they look. When they fail us or fall short of our expectation, we withdraw our honor, and this leads to hurt and offense. When left unaddressed, hurting people hurt others and before we know it, we are left with a kingdom of hurting and wounded people. Having a vibrant relationship with the Spirit of God gives us the strength to honor others despite their character weaknesses or personality flaws because we honor God Himself. Above and beyond that, the Holy Spirit gives us the divine knowledge to understand God's heart for them and the divine insight into their journeys so that we can continue to have compassion for them.

(B) The Spirit of Wisdom and Understanding

Proverbs 3:7 instructs us that amongst all our getting, we must get wisdom and understanding. The Holy Spirit is the giver of such wisdom and understanding. **Wisdom brings discernment**, which is having God's perception or insight into a particular situation. Discernment helps us recognize good from bad, right from wrong, and true from false. James 3:17 describes the wisdom from above as first pure, then peaceable, gentle, willing to yield, full of mercy, and bears good fruits, without partiality, and without hypocrisy. When we have God's discernment, we can make decisions to preserve good relationships or redraw boundaries for unhealthy ones in a way that will bring peace and not offense. **Wisdom gives discretion.** Once we have wisdom, discretion will protect us, and understanding will guard us. Proverbs 5:1-2 says, *"My son, pay attention to my wisdom, listen well to my words of insight, that you may maintain discretion."* Discretion is the wisdom to know when to speak or act and when to hold back. It gives us the ability to not give into gossiping and slandering when we are wronged, thereby disallowing demons to entrap us.

Wisdom gives direction. Wisdom helps us make good choices that will direct our relationships to the place of peace, joy, and mutual blessings. Proverbs 14:1 says, *"The wise woman builds her house, but the foolish pulls it down with her hands."* Wisdom is necessary for leadership, and leadership is influence. That influence is independent of title or sometimes even position. We can influence one another and lead in different dynamics and situations. Therefore, we must find wisdom in our relationships so that we can see progress and not destruction.

(C) The Spirit of Counsel and Might

Every meaningful relationship exists to bring comfort and joy and to inspire a change, hopefully for the better. While in relationship, we often find ourselves in a place where we are in need of counsel or giving counsel. With the Holy Spirit's help, we can provide counsel from the perspective of God and lead our friends and family to the place of order and blessings and not to the place of chaos and more trouble. We can lend our strength to those who are weak and encourage them to choose the narrow path even though it may be difficult. That is why God cautions us not to walk with the ungodly, stand in the paths of sinners, nor sit with the scornful. Especially when we are in a valley and our thoughts are clouded and eyes blurred by our plight, we need godly people who have the wisdom of counsel and the strength to tell us what we need to hear and not what we want to hear.

Psalm 1:1-3

Blessed is the man
Who walks not in the counsel of the ungodly,
Nor stands in the path of sinners,
Nor sits in the seat of the scornful;
But his delight is in the law of the Lord,
And in His law, he meditates day and night.
He shall be like a tree
Planted by the rivers of water,

That brings forth its fruit in its season,
Whose leaf also shall not wither;
And whatever he does shall prosper.

Hence, we need the Holy Spirit to bring counsel and might to heal our hearts and restore relationships. Zechariah 4:6 states that the Spirit of God helps us achieve what we cannot do by our might or power. He'll help you through crises. He'll show you what to do in every situation in your personal life, relationships, ministry, business, and more. The word "might" literally means powerful, strong, and valiant. It is used to describe a proven warrior. It is the same word used to describe the Lord in Psalm 24:7-8.

Psalm 24:7-8

Lift up your heads, O you gates! And be lifted up, you everlasting doors! And the King of glory shall come in. Who is this King of glory? The Lord strong and mighty, the Lord mighty in battle.

So, we need the Holy Spirit of might. We need the Holy Spirit, the Mighty One of Israel (Isa. 1:24). He is filled with valor, and His ability to win in battle is proven. He is the victor 100 percent of the time. He has never lost a battle He has taken on, and He never will. As a woman of God who desires to prepare the way for the return of the Lord, partnership with the Holy Spirit is not optional but essential.

The Partnership with the Holy Spirit

Every woman is an extension of the story of Eve, and what the first Eve could not do, the Second Eve must achieve. However, without the Holy Spirit, the works of God would not be made possible.

Eve The Last

Without the Spirit of God, we can do nothing. We are as ships without the wind, or chariots without steeds; like branches without sap, we are withered; like coals without fire, we are useless; as an offering without the sacrificial flame, we are unaccepted.

— Charles Spurgeon (1834–1892)

Charles Spurgeon, a nineteenth-century English Baptist minister and one of the most influential, extraordinary preachers of his era, acknowledged that without the Holy Spirit's help we would be useless. He echoed Zechariah 4:6.

Zechariah 4:6

"Not by might nor by power, but by My Spirit," says the Lord of hosts.

Let us embark on this journey to know the Holy Spirit, to be familiar with His leading, to be fully endowed with His power. In doing so, we will fulfill the design of God for every woman, to live as a gift, fight like a warrior, operate in the anointing of the Holy Spirit, and love with the heart of a mother. May we arise and continue the story of Eve and let the Author finish our story, the story of the Last Eve.

Chapter 10

The Last Eve

Ephesians 5:31-33

"For this reason a man shall leave his father and mother and be joined to his wife, and the two shall become one flesh." This is a great mystery, but I speak concerning Christ and the church. Nevertheless let each one of you in particular so love his own wife as himself, and let the wife see that she respects her husband.

P aul, in reference to the Scriptures, draws a parallel between the relationship of Christ and the church to that of a marriage relationship between a husband and a wife. In his writing to the Corinthian church, he emphasized that *"woman was made for man"* (1 Cor. 11:9). This is ultimately true because the church is made for Christ (Rev. 21:2). In the fifteenth chapter of the same letter to the Corinthian church, Paul addresses the subject of the exchange that happens in the resurrection of the dead by referring to the Lord as the *"Last Adam"* (1 Cor. 15:45). In conclusion, the church is the bride of Christ, the (last) New Adam's (last) New Eve.

Eve The Last

God has joined us to Himself in an everlasting covenant. We, the church, are now flesh of Christ's flesh and bone of Christ's bones. Man and woman now form the church; both symbolize the "woman" or the "New Eve" in the big picture. However, from a more microperspective, if every man represents Christ in a marriage relationship then every woman truly represents the "New Eve." Although woman came from man, we are made of the same material and given the same mandate to have dominion over the creations of God. Men and women, together, manifest the full likeness and glory of our Creator. However, men and women have different roles and assume different authorities. But one cannot perform his or her role without the other. In some ways, this is reflected in the game of chess.

In chess, the queen has more freedom (mobility) on the chessboard. The king is the most important piece of the set and must be protected. The game is based on the premise that a monarchy will be destroyed when a king is destroyed. The king piece can only move one step at a time, which makes him vulnerable. Strategy in chess must revolve around not only attacking your opponent's king but also protecting your own king. The queen is the second most important piece and is very valuable because she can move in several directions and ways. This makes the queen a useful piece that can be used for annihilating other players. At the same time, if your queen is destroyed, then you lose this advantage in the game.

God has set in creation for men to carry the authority and the anointing of the headship. Although women seem to play "second fiddle" to men, God has given women great spiritual mobility; and if women fully recognized their design and assumed their power, they would be a great advantage to men. Without this female insight, men would likely be exposed to demonic attacks due to having a "spiritual blind side." Earlier chapters expressed how principalities that are set to come against the church seek to destroy the headship authority that is upon every man in our society. So often, these powers of darkness work through women whose hearts are wounded and have a vendetta against men.

Revelation 19:1-8

After these things I heard a loud voice of a great multitude in heaven, saying, "Alleluia! Salvation and glory and honor and power belong to the Lord our God! For true and righteous are His judgments, because He has judged the **great harlot who corrupted the earth with her fornication; and He has avenged on her the blood of His servants shed by her."** *Again they said, "Alleluia! Her smoke rises up forever and ever!" And the twenty-four elders and the four living creatures fell down and worshiped God who sat on the throne, saying, "Amen! Alleluia!" Then a voice came from the throne, saying, "Praise our God, all you His servants and those who fear Him, both small and great!" And I heard, as it were, the voice of a great multitude, as the sound of many waters and as the sound of mighty thundering, saying, "Alleluia! For the Lord God Omnipotent reigns! Let us be glad and rejoice and give Him glory, for the marriage of the Lamb has come, and* **His wife has made herself ready**.*" And to her it was granted to be arrayed in fine linen, clean and bright, for the fine linen is the righteous acts of the saints.*

Revelation 19 talks about two women: the great harlot that God will judge and the wife that God will rejoice. And when He returns, He will find the latter *"arrayed in fine linen which is the righteous acts of the saints."* As the "New Eve" for the Lord, how can the woman of God prepare for the return of the One whom she loves? I

We must develop ourselves to be the reflection of the W.H.O.L.E. womanhood of God.

believe we must develop ourselves to be the reflection of the W.H.O.L.E. womanhood of God.

W: Word, Wisdom, Worth

Word. The Last Eve loves the Word of God and abides by the Word in her life, just like Mary of Bethany, who was often found at the feet of Jesus, leaning into every Word spoken by the Lord. The Last Eve considers the Word before she considers her circumstances. She chooses to yield to the Word before she yields to her emotions. She yearns to hear the Lord's voice and lives to fulfill His Word.

Matthew 4:4

But He answered and said, "It is written, 'Man shall not live by bread alone, but by every word that proceeds from the mouth of God.'"

Wisdom. Her wisdom comes from above, and she desires to bring kingdom order to every relationship and situation she is in. The Bible mentions two wise women: The Wise Woman of Tekoa (2 Sam. 14) and The Wise Woman of Abel-beth-maachah (2 Sam. 20). Both women acted wisely and authoritatively. Their advice, which was heeded by powerful men—King David in the first instance and Joab in the second— prevented the former from losing his honor and in the latter, saved him from a disastrous decision that would have caused a massive massacre.

Job 28:28

Behold, the fear of the Lord, that is wisdom,
And to depart from evil is understanding.

Worth. The Last Eve is grounded in the full revelation of her worth. Her identity is found in her Heavenly Father who birthed her.

Her worth is rooted in the fact that Jesus abandoned all to redeem her. Because of that, she does not envy others and is not jealous of any other woman because she knows that she is uniquely created and fearfully made. Living free from a need to prove herself, she can fully develop herself and hence be a blessing to her husband, children, and the people who are connected to her life (Prov. 31:10-31).

Proverbs 31:10

Who can find a virtuous wife?
For her worth is far above rubies.

H: Holy, (full of the) Holy Spirit, Hospitable

Holy. Whether in the Greek word *"hagios"* or the Hebrew word *"qodesh,"* "holy" means pretty much the same—"apartness, sacredness" or "being set apart"—showing that God is altogether holy, sacred, set apart, or separate from His creation.

The Word of God instructs us to be holy just as God is holy. Part of that growth toward holiness is not being conformed to this world (Rom. 12:1-2) and is an ongoing lifetime process called sanctification or to be set apart for holy use. The Last Eve is committed to living for Christ and being set apart for His purpose and plan. She deliberately chooses to be a subject in His kingdom. Like Rahab, she is willing to abandon all to follow Jesus. Although Rahab did not have the most flattering profession, she was wise enough to recognize that the God of the Israelites was the only God! In that critical moment of history, she rightly feared God and made a radical decision to abandon her god and way of life to embrace the true and living God and adopt the culture of the kingdom. Not only did she save the day but she, through her abandonment, saved her family and became grafted into the lineage of Jesus Christ (Josh. 2, 6; Matt. 1:5)!

Matthew 16:24

Then Jesus said to His disciples, "If anyone desires to come after Me, let him deny himself, and take up his cross, and follow Me."

Holy Spirit. The Holy Spirit's role in a believer's life is extremely critical to prepare them for spiritual maturity, influence, and authority. The Last Eve fully understands the Purpose of the Holy Spirit in her life and yields to His Power. She reveres the Person of the Holy Spirit and seeks to be a carrier of His Presence. In the things she says and does, she desires to be the extension of His work. In 2 Kings 22, Huldah is the only female prophet in the book of Kings. When King Josiah had questions about the book of the Law that was found, his priest, secretary, and attendant went to see Huldah to clarify God's Word. They trusted that Huldah would prophesy the truth and knew that she heard from God. The Last Eve hears from the Holy Spirit and is free from religiosity.

Galatians 5:17-18

For the flesh lusts against the Spirit, and the Spirit against the flesh; and these are contrary to one another, so that you do not do the things that you wish. But if you are led by the Spirit, you are not under the law.

Hospitable. Hospitality is a virtue that is both commanded and commended throughout Scripture. This virtue is seen more often in a woman who is designed to be relational and carry the heart of a mother, whether married or single. The Last Eve is one who welcomes people not only in her home but also in her heart. Her heart is big enough to contain the people that the Lord would give to her. In Acts 16:14-15, we read about Lydia, one of the first woman converts to Christianity.

She was described as a worshipper of God and a businesswoman with a family. Upon her conversion and baptism, she passionately pursued God and relationship with His people. Though she was apparently wealthy, she humbled herself by offering hospitality to others.

Titus 1:7-9

For a bishop must be blameless, as a steward of God, not self-willed, not quick-tempered, not given to wine, not violent, not greedy for money, but hospitable, a lover of what is good, sober-minded, just, holy, self-controlled, holding fast the faithful word as he has been taught, that he may be able, by sound doctrine, both to exhort and convict those who contradict.

O: One with God and His People

One with God. Colossians 1 speaks of Jesus reconciling us to Him through the blood. We, who were once alienated because of our evil conscience, are now made holy and blameless and above reproach in His sight. In the Old Testament, the word reconciliation is the Hebrew word "kapar." This is one of the most theologically significant words in the Bible. In addition to reconciliation, *"kapar"* is also translated into English words such as forgive, purge away, and merciful, as well as a few others. By far, the most commonly translated word for kapar is the English word "atonement."

> **Through this abiding relationship with Christ, she finds her fruitfulness in the things she labors and builds.**

AT-ONE-ment = To be reconciled means to be made "at one" with God.

Eve The Last

To lead a powerful Christian life, the Last Eve must learn to dwell as one with her Creator. This "oneness" is the source of her authority and influence. Through this abiding relationship with Christ, she finds her fruitfulness in the things she labors and builds.

John 15:5

I am the vine; you are the branches. He who abides in Me, and I in him, bears much fruit; for without Me you can do nothing.

Because of this "oneness" with Christ, the Last Eve is a picture of complete loyalty to God and all that He seeks to accomplish. Her loyalty extends beyond the local church or her ministry. She is loyal to the kingdom and sees her ministry in the local church as part of the big picture of making His kingdom prosperous and visible. The story of Ruth symbolizes such loyalty. When her Jewish mother-in-law Naomi returned to Israel from Moab, Ruth stuck with her and pledged to follow Naomi and worship her God. Because of her loyalty to Naomi, Ruth embraced a new way of living and followed a new culture. By her reputation of loyalty, Boaz, a kindly landowner, exercised his right as kinsman-redeemer to marry Ruth and rescue both women from poverty. Through her marriage to Boaz, according to Matthew, Ruth became an ancestor of King David, whose descendant was Jesus Christ.

Ruth 1:16

But Ruth said: "Entreat me not to leave you, Or to turn back from following after you; For wherever you go, I will go; And wherever you lodge, I will lodge; Your people shall be my people, And your God, my God."

Today, the Lord is still looking for men and women who will not turn back from following Him. The Last Eve has the cross before her and the world behind her. She will go where He goes and lodge where He lodges. Her heart is loyal before Him so that He can display His glory over her life.

2 Chronicles 16:9

For the eyes of the Lord run to and from throughout the whole earth, to show Himself strong on behalf of those whose heart is loyal to Him. In this you have done foolishly; therefore, from now on you shall have wars.

In today's controversial world, being loyal to Christ may well land you in unpopular places with your friends and family. You will find yourself making some difficult decisions because you are going against the culture of your time. For example, the decision to live a life of purity and uphold sexual abstinence before marriage, though noble in times past, is now deemed "old-fashion" or "being religious." The Bible instructs the wife to be submitted to her husband and unto the Lord, a picture of the extension of "being one" with God.

Instead of being celebrated as a life surrendered to Christ, in some cultures and more prominently so in America, it is frowned upon as being "weak" or "unliberated." The Last Eve who is one with Christ is not only loyal, she is brave. She is not afraid to be branded as counter-cultural when the world's culture conflicts with that of the kingdom of God. In the story of Jehosheba (2 Kings 11:2-3), Jehosheba risked her life to save Prince Joash when his grandmother, Athaliah, in a bid to secure her position, went on a rampage to execute the entire royal family. Through Jehosheba's bravery and love, this seemingly ordinary woman saved the royal line of King David from extinction.

1 Corinthians 16:13

Watch, stand fast in the faith, be brave, be strong.

Eve The Last

Quite commonly as women, we fear other people's opinions of us. We are constantly afraid to be misunderstood or for some people to see our "true colors." Although the Last Eve may battle with fears and apprehensions, she is apprehended by the reverential fear for the Lord. Hence, she would choose what is right and not what feels right no matter how difficult, just like Shiphrah and Puah in Exodus 1. These two Hebrew midwives feared God more than the unnamed pharaoh in Egypt; this pharaoh had ordered all Hebrew baby boys be killed in order to contain the growth of the children of Israelites. Instead of caving in to the pharaoh's command, through wittiness these midwives saved many Hebrew children's lives, which led to the growing number of God's chosen people even during the time of slavery.

1 Peter 2:17

Honor all people. Love the brotherhood. Fear God. Honor the king.

One with His People. The evidence of the Last Eve's oneness with God is in her being also one with the body of Christ. God's love for the church is a revelation that propels her to fight for the church and to do all that she can for the people that make up the church. She is loyal to her local church, but she is faithful to the body of believers regardless of language, culture, and color. Queen Esther's loyalty to Mordecai, her uncle, (and ultimately to God) caused her to risk her life to save the Jewish people from destruction, protecting the line of the future Savior, Jesus Christ. She was selected in a beauty pageant to become queen to the Persian King Xerxes. However, a wicked court official, Haman, plotted to have all the Jews murdered. Esther's uncle Mordecai convinced her to approach the king and tell him the truth. The tables quickly turned when Haman was hanged on the gallows meant for Mordecai. The royal order was overridden, and Mordecai won Haman's job. The Last Eve is loyal to God and has a strong alliance to the Church. She seeks the overall wellness of the people of God, not just her own comfort and success. She fights to see the manifestation of the glory of God on His people and is not afraid to sacrifice to see His will be done, enough to utter the famous words of Queen Esther, *"If I perish, I perish!"*

L: Leadership

From the onset of creation, man was mandated to create culture and build civilization (Gen. 1:28). Today, we refer to this as the "cultural mandate," which is the mandate to "develop the social order" and "harness the natural world" according to God's intention. However, due to the fall of man and the corruptions of our hearts and minds, what we harnessed from the natural world was not put to its intended use. God then had to bring restoration to fallen humanity and our fallen world. To reveal His intention, He revealed His name, "Yahweh," which means God, the Redeemer (Exod. 3:13-14). Redemption is the conversion of man to restore the kingdom order, influence, and authority so that men can use their God-given creativity and talent to harness the world for the good of society. To do that, we need a major paradigm shift in the body of Christ today regarding leadership! To bring about change, the right people must lead!

Matthew 5:13-16

You are the salt of the earth; but if the salt loses its flavor, how shall it be seasoned? It is then good for nothing but to be thrown out and trampled underfoot by men. You are the light of the world. A city that is set on a hill cannot be hidden. Nor do they light a lamp and put it under a basket, but on a lampstand, and it gives light to all who are in the house. Let your light so shine before men, that they may see your good works and glorify your Father in heaven.

Eve The Last

Salt speaks of healing and redemption. Light helps us see the way to that redemption. Believers who desire to change the world must follow the way of Jesus. He is a Servant and a King. He is the Savior and the Lord. He follows the Father and leads the change! In a similar manner, believers must learn to be followers of Jesus and lead the rest of humanity to redemption. Because the church has neglected to continuously develop God's social order, the world is now broken. Different social orders have replaced God's order, and we see a rapid spiraling down of moral standards, healthy relationships, and living qualities.

What have we, the church, tolerated? We have tolerated dishonor, sexual immorality, divorce, and many degradations of our faith by failing to teach the people the full counsel of God's Word. Instead, we have allowed the liberal teaching of grace to give us a license to live a lawless lifestyle and, in the name of love, gag our mouths and lose our authority to speak against these violations.

Are we willing to tolerate this chaos? God will not change what you are willing to tolerate. In fact, what you tolerate will dominate. Wayne Cordeiro, author of *Leading on Empty*, wrote, "When your car's in neutral, anybody can push it around." It is urgent that we do not stay neutral on the issues that plague the church and that we start getting this big ship to go where it needs to be and accomplish what God is desiring to see—just like the Bible says, "especially when you see the Day fast approaching."

We must lead the change we need to see in the social world by changing one person at a time through making disciples. This is in accordance with the great commission that the Lord commanded. However, the greatest obstacle to this is that most believers lack a leader's mindset!

"Is everyone a leader?"

Yes and no. It all depends on how you define "leader." If you define it in the traditional fashion—that a leader is someone in charge of a group of people in an organization—then the answer is no, in my opinion. Not everyone is gifted to become the president, the chairman, the CEO, or the key leader of a large team of people. Most will never occupy a top spot in a flow chart; perhaps only 10 percent of the population will.

If we define leadership in a different manner, it opens up an entirely new perspective. What if leadership was more about people pursuing a "calling" in life, a calling with which we will influence others in its fulfillment? What if leadership had more to do with finding an area of strength—and in using that strength, we naturally influenced others in a positive way? If leadership is about using our influence for a worthwhile cause, then Christian leadership is about using our influence for the cause of Christ!

Matthew 28:19

Go therefore and make disciples of all the nations, baptizing them in the name of the Father and of the Son and of the Holy Spirit …

2 Corinthians 5:11 (AMP)

Therefore, since we know the fear of the Lord [and understand the importance of obedience and worship], we persuade people [to be reconciled to Him].

This means a mature follower of Christ will eventually become a leader of people. A believer is a leader to some extent and degree! Part of what it means to be made in God's image is that people have the capacity to lead and rule. You will always be following, and you will also be leading. The Bible talks about a woman leader, Phoebe, who was outstanding in influencing the work of the ministry. Phoebe was a deacon who served with the overseers of the church. Due to the culture of that time, women were not readily given leadership roles. But Phoebe was so outstanding as a deacon that Paul singled her out in Romans

16:1-2 and highlighted how she had been a benefactor for him and many others. No mention is made of her husband, if she had one.

The Last Eve embraces her gift to lead. She is keen to learn to lead and influence in a manner appropriate with her giftedness and not excuse herself because she's never going to be like Mother Teresa or Christine Caine. She knows that leadership is about becoming the person we were meant to be. It is less about position and more about disposition. It is not so much about superiority but about service in the area of our strengths. It has less to do with a set of behaviors and more to do with a perspective with which we view life. She is one who knows how to follow and has earned the right to lead.

E: Engagement at Home, in the Marketplace, and in the Church

Just like a man, a woman is created with gifts that cause her to be a valuable player wherever she goes, whether in the family, in church, in society, or in the marketplace. Embracing fully how God has designed us to be, we should not draw back from engaging in any arena and serve wholeheartedly with our gifts and talents. God desires to see us apply ourselves fully to build His social order and to harness the world that God has created so that we can be a blessing to the world. We should not and must not draw back because in Hebrews 10:38, God specifically says that His soul has no pleasure in him (her) who draws back. Created to complement the men in our generation, we can see the manifestation of God's dominion as mandated in Genesis if we know how to work effectively together. The result of that would be fruitfulness and glory.

At Home. Whether you are a full-time mom or a working mom, your presence in your family is instrumental for the emotional well-being of your children as well as your husband. Mothers are the emotional backbones of the family. Married or otherwise, the Last Eve carries the *"incorruptible beauty of a gentle and quiet spirit, which is very precious in the sight of God"* (1 Pet. 3:4). She seeks to care for and be a blessing to the people she connects with (Prov. 31:15), constantly bringing reconciliation in these relationships. She labors to turn the hearts of the fathers to the children and the hearts of the children to their fathers (Mal. 4:6) and not turn them against each other. She does not resist her husband's authority and grows in willing submission to her husband's leadership regardless of the imperfection of that leadership (Col. 3:18-19). She can do so because she first submits to the Lord she loves and knows that God sees every-thing and is the judge over all things. She watches over the ways of her household (Prov. 31:27) and ensures that the children are trained up in the way they should go (Prov. 22:6).

In the Marketplace. *Businesswoman Media* cites three reasons why women are effective workers in the business world: Women not only learn better, but they communicate better and are more engaged as employees and leaders.[1] The Last Eve knows how to use her spiritual and natural gifts and talents to work effectively and bring about the results she wants to see in her work and also in the people with whom she works. She sees her workplace as her mission field and is sensitive to partner with the Holy Spirit to bring healing and reconciliation to her business peers. She honors everyone, which includes her bosses and her coworkers (1 Pet. 2:17). She sees people as the ones whom God loves regardless of their religion or lifestyle. She is diligent with her hands and through her faithfulness becomes a source of provision for others (Prov. 31:24-25, 27).

In the Church. In the church, sin pushes men toward a worldly love of power or an abdication of spiritual responsibility. This causes

---

[1]   https://www.thebusinesswomanmedia.com/3-reasons-women-better-employees

women to resist limitations on their roles or to neglect the use of their gifts in appropriate ministries. The Last Eve understands her purpose and fully embraces her role, yet never covets for what is not hers (Luke 12:15). She does not strive to promote herself or her ministry but uses her God-given gifts and skills to work with the men to move the kingdom of God forward (Matt. 6:33). She develops a mature spiritual discernment between what is God and what is not (Col. 2:8). She resists against the works of demons and refuses to participate in their attempt to cause her to break covenant with God and with the people whom God has ordained, especially the men (Eph. 6:12). She honors the headship in the church and seeks to protect it and not usurp or undermine its authority, which comes from God (Heb. 13:17).

Acts 18:3 shows a great example of how the Last Eve serves alongside her husband in ministry. They are the power couple Pricilla and Aquila, who were tentmakers. It is significant to note that Priscilla is always mentioned with her husband and never on her own. However, they are always shown as equals in Christ, and the two of them together are remembered as leaders of the early church. Paul, in Romans 16:3-4, made special mention of how this couple risked their lives for him, and Luke in Acts 18 remarked that they were instrumental in helping Apollos understand the gospel message of Jesus Christ. Priscilla and Aquila represent how a husband and wife can have an equal partnership in their work for the Lord. Priscilla was noted for having equal importance to her husband, both to God and the early church. The Last Eve is ready to work alongside the men in her arena, be it at home, in the marketplace, or in the ministry. A clarion example is Deborah in the Old Testament (Judg. 4-5).

Deborah played a unique role in Israel's history. She served as the only female judge in a lawless period before the country got its first king. In Israel's male-dominated culture of that time, it was unimaginable for a woman to instruct a man, let alone to judge a nation! Women were not educated, so how did Deborah know the law to apply it in the situations she judged? We can only deduce that her father or very likely her husband taught her. Of course, God had clearly anointed her with divine wisdom and the people could not deny the call on her life, so they all submitted under her rule; that included even the mighty warrior Barak. Through Deborah's prophetic insight, Barak defeated the oppressive general Sisera, not without first insisting that Deborah come along in the battle. Deborah did not take this opportunity to promote herself or put him down. Instead, she cautioned him about the possible consequence of the people crediting the victory to her instead of Barak. Deborah's heart is not to highlight her position, but she sees herself as one with the rulers of God whose main ministry is to serve His people.

Judges 5:9

My heart is with the rulers of Israel
Who offered themselves willingly with the people.
Bless the Lord!

This is a beautiful picture of how man and woman must stand together to fight against the enemies that have come to attack the kingdom of God and destroy His people. God is raising up a generation of New Eves who will not emasculate the men but will fight for their headship. The women warriors are the frontline defense for the church, using their prophetic inclination to pray against the schemes of demons. Through their discernment, they will disarm powers of darkness such as the works of Jezebel, Leviathan, and Absalom so that the men can rise up in their spiritual vision and strength to lead the kingdom of God to the place God intends before the Lord returns. Together with Deborah, Barak was able to defeat the army of Sisera. However, Sisera was killed by another woman, Jael, who drove a tent stake through his head while

> The smallness you feel comes from within you. Your lives aren't small, but you're living them in a small way. I'm speaking as plainly as I can and with great affection. Open up your lives. Live openly and expansively!

he was sleeping. Thanks to Deborah's leadership, Israel enjoyed peace for forty years.

Judges 5:7

Village life ceased, it ceased in Israel,
Until I, Deborah, arose ...

We are entering a very tumultuous era, yet there awaits great adventures for the women of God who would arise just like Deborah. Will you start this journey to allow God to remake you and transform you into the Last Eve that would be the perfect bride for the Last Adam, a woman who knows her worth through the Word? She walks in wisdom from above. She is hospitable because she loves. She is one with God through the works of the Holy Spirit. She leads with strength and grace and engages her world with an open heart and open arms. She stands without fear beside the men and sees His kingdom come, His will be done! May the Last Eve arise!

Friends, as Paul prayed in 2 Corinthians 6:11-13, my prayer for you is also that you would "enter this wide-open, spacious life. We didn't fence you in. The smallness you feel comes from within you. Your lives aren't small, but you're living them in a small way. I'm speaking as plainly as I can and with great affection. Open up your lives. Live openly and expansively!"

Author Contact

If you would like to contact Susan Dunn, find out more information, purchase books, or request her to speak, please contact:

Susan Dunn

(949) 265-0440

derekdunn.org

wow31@derekdunn.org

Follow Susan on Facebook: @wow31livefreelovestrong and Instagram: @wow31ministry.

www.ingramcontent.com/pod-product-compliance
Lightning Source LLC
Chambersburg PA
CBHW070620100426
42744CB00006B/554